LIVING
LIFE
INTENTIONALLY

LIVING
LIFE
INTENTIONALLY

Richard W. Luecke

Lucky Learning, Inc.
Cleveland, Ohio

Living Life Intentionally
Copyright © 1996 by Richard W. Luecke. All rights reserved.

No part of this book may be quoted in any form (printed, written, visual, electronic, or audio) without written permission of the publisher.

Cover Design: Don Borger
Interior Layout: Brian Stash

Library of Congress Catalog Card Number 96-94791
  Luecke, Richard W.
    Living Life Intentionally / by Richard W. Luecke

ISBN 1-889774-02-2

Printed in the United States of America

1 2 3 4 5 99 98 97 96

CONTENTS

Dedication ix
Acknowledgments xi
Foreword xiii
Introduction xv

1. Against All Odds 1
2. "All I Am Or Ever Hope To Be, I Owe..." 3
3. On Being Aggressive 6
4. Trust—The Key Ingredient 8
5. Confidence 15
6. Guaranteed Stagnation 18
7. "Today I Begin A New Life" 20
8. Focus 23
9. Learned Optimism 25
10. Interview Technique #1: Building Trust 28
11. Total Integrity 30
12. Carpe Diem 33
13. Leading By Example 36
14. "Nice Guys Finish Last" 39
15. Health And Fitness 42
16. Listening 46
17. What Your Customers Really Buy 49
18. A Self-Fulfilling Prophecy 51
19. Interview Technique #2: Advancing 54
20. "I Will Greet This Day with Love In My Heart" 59
21. Invite Dissent 62
22. Ten Ways To Self-Destruct 64
23. What's Your Failure Rate? 65
24. Take This Job And . . . Love It! 68
25. Reflections... 71
26. "I Will Persist Until I Succeed" 75
27. "No Excuse, Sir!" 78
28. Interview Technique #3: Fact Finding 81
29. "... And Then Some" 86
30. Smooth Sailing 88
31. A New King Of Patriot 90
32. "... And The Times They Are A Changin" 93

33.	Integrity: Your Code Of Ethics	99
34.	Interview Technique #4: Recommendations	102
35.	"I Am Nature's Greatest Miracle"	106
36.	Tradition	109
37.	Building Long Term Relationships	112
38.	On Risking	114
39.	We Believe	117
40.	"I Will Live This Day As If It Is My Last"	122
41.	Good Advice	125
42.	Delayed Gratification	128
43.	Faithfulness	134
44.	Interview Technique #5: Closing	137
45.	Independence—Bane Or Blessing?	140
46.	Has This Cost You A Sale Recently?	143
47.	Marketing Trends	145
48.	"Today I Will Be Master Of My Emotions"	148
49.	Amazing Service	152
50.	Time To Sacrifice The Queen?	155
51.	Presence	161
52.	Opportunities Abound	164
53.	"I Will Laugh At The World"	168
54.	An Inconvenience...Or A Problem?	171
55.	Thank God It's Wednesday (TGIW)	177
56.	Persistence	180
57.	Hula Hoops and Frisbees	183
58.	Courageous Conversations	186
59.	Are You Indispensable?	189
60.	Differentiation	192
61.	Joe Average	195
62.	"No One Has Endurance Like . . ."	201
63.	"Today I Will Multiply My Value A Hundredfold" . .	204
64.	Just Do It!	206
65.	Customize And Personalize	213
66.	Ten Steps For Better Listening	.215
67.	A Lesson in Brevity	217
68.	Solutions Not Ingredients	218
69.	"What Do You Expect?"	220
70.	Interview Technique #6: Follow-up	223

71.	Image Problem?	226
72.	And The Winner Is...	229
73.	Caveat Emptor—Let The Buyer Beware	232
74.	No Pain; No Gain	236
75.	Grandmothers Are Special People	239
76.	Courage	245
77.	Looking The Part	249
78.	"I Will Act Now"	253
79.	The Buck Stops Here	259
80.	A Blinding Glimpse Of The Obvious	262
81.	Your Valuable Time	267
82.	On Being Coachable	269

DEDICATION

I dedicate this book to my wife, Linda. Her love and devotion have made this journey through life interesting, memorable and joyful. To her I owe everything.

ACKNOWLEDGMENTS

A project of this nature is never an individual effort accomplished by one person. Rather, it will be difficult to recognize all the people who have contributed in one way or another to its completion. First, and as always foremost, I'd like to thank my best friend, my wife Linda, for her encouragement, nurturing and constant love. She has been the best person in my life. I'd also like to thank my parents, Walter and Frieda Luecke, and brother, Randy Luecke, for all the ways they have contributed to bring this book about. The values and principles they promote and live are not only recorded in these pages, but are indelibly written on my heart. I love them dearly.

A huge "thank you" also goes to Judy Marinko whose countless hours of recording, changing, re-typing, re-doing, and manuscript writing was always done willingly, cheerfully and most often times enthusiastically. Her loyalty, support and encouragement have always been appreciated. She continues to be an appreciated sounding board, confidante, professional administrative assistant and friend. She is dependable beyond description.

Others who I want to thank are Judy Gesch, Marcus Fish, Jennifer Marinko, and again my Dad, Walter Luecke, for their suggestions, encouragement and editing. I owe a huge amount of gratitude to Brian Stash for his relentless time and effort in preparing the manuscript to be printed. To my best friend (next to Linda) of almost 40 years, John Fish, I say "thank you" for your many contributions to this effort (especially Chapter 8 entitled "Focus" which was principally his thoughts). Howard Wight has also been supportive every step of the way and I want to thank him. Thanks too, Howard, for writing the Foreword. I'd also like to thank George Qua who has not only been a mentor and friend, but a person who more than anyone else encouraged me to write this book.

One other person needs mentioning. My brother, Bob, while not with us since 1968 (see Chapter 25 entitled "Reflections"), has contributed to this book in a number of ways. He was a gifted writer, my early hero and role model in life, and he continues to inspire me today. Thanks Bob!

To all the others who have contributed in one way or another to this book (especially those to whom I dedicate a chapter!) I say "thanks". My apologies to anyone I have inadvertently omitted.

Foreword

Dick Luecke's *Living Life Intentionally* will help you become a winner in selling and in life. Success is about making a difference . . . not just about making money. Most people don't understand that. Those who make the biggest difference in the lives of others are those who have a mission . . . a purpose. Each of us is given a gift. Our job in life is to find our gift and then to share it with others. Knowing that you have a mission, you can then live life intentionally . . . focusing on serving others.

This is a book to savor. Every single chapter contains a gem which you will treasure. Read this book, and then re-read it. I suggest that you read it in its entirety initially, and then read one chapter each day before you start work. Repetition is the key to learning, skill, competence, expertise, and ultimately to mastery.

Successful people consistently do what others can do but don't. Dick will provide you with the tools and techniques required to become an outstanding salesperson and individual. More importantly, he emphasizes the rewards and results of relationships. Nobody becomes a success on his or her own. We become successful because of our relationships with our families, our friends, our clients, our associates, and countless others whose paths cross ours.

When you start to understand the importance of relationships, you begin to realize the importance of working with people you care about and who care about their families and employees. Life is too short to work with people who don't care. Trying to sell someone who doesn't care is like trying to teach a pig to sing. It annoys the pig, and it wastes your time.

Most of us at some point in our lives ask ourselves, "Why am I here?" Dick Luecke will help you answer that question. I wish you success in life and in selling. Let Dick Luecke become a part of the dream team which helps you achieve your dreams. Let him help you help others convert their dreams to reality. Make your life a mission . . . not just a job or a career. Live your life intentionally . . . with purpose.

Howard Wight
Summer 1996

Introduction

Living Life Intentionally is designed to help you live your life more successfully. Its short insightful messages are aimed at helping you stay focused and on purpose. Everyone can gain from the practical and useful ideas presented.

Intentional living has been easier for me since I've had cancer. Life is more precious now. Every moment seems more valuable. No more meadering through life with no real goals. No more passive living. My hope is that these messages will challenge you to live your life more intentionally.

Contained in the messages in each chapter are nuggets of insight and gems of truth that will reinforce your values and convictions. While the ideas may not be revolutionary, they will serve as reminders of concepts and perceptions that will lead to a more successful life.

Life is not a dress rehearsal—so live your life intentionally! Good luck!

Chapter 1

AGAINST ALL ODDS

"The difference between the possible and the impossible lies in the man's determination."
— Tommy Lasorda

It's amazing what we can learn from even the smallest of God's creatures. Take the bumblebee for example. The average hive houses from 30,000 to 60,000 bees. The queen lays anywhere from 1,500 to 2,000 eggs per day during the summer. The bumblebee's life expectancy is less than one year. These are the tasks of the bumblebee:

Days 1-2	Clean the hive
Days 3-9	Feed the larvae (larvae must be fed 1,300 times per day)
Days 10-16	Receive food from "field" bees and store in cells
Days 17-20	Guard the hive
Days 21 & After	Full-fledged "field" bee - gather food

There are probably many little lessons in life in this "order" of responsibilities and tasks. But of all the lessons, the lesson I like best about the bumblebee is this one:

According to the laws of aerodynamics, the bumblebee cannot fly.

I guess no one bothered to tell the bee! CNN didn't report it on their nightly news program. There were no headlines in the newspaper, **"Bumblebee Can't Fly!",** and the government never issued a 300 page report indicating that it's impossible for the bumblebee to fly.

Isn't that great?! It reminds me of the Confucius saying, "Person who say it cannot be done should not interrupt person doing it."

What a lesson! **Don't listen to skeptics and critics who tell you something can't be done.** Just do it! There may be any number of legitimate reasons (excuses) why you cannot accomplish a goal. Go out and do it anyway! **No one knows your resolve, so don't let anyone influence your thinking.** If one of the smallest of God's creatures can overcome unbelievable odds, just think what the greatest of God's creations can accomplish!

Chapter 2

"ALL I AM OR EVER HOPE TO BE, I OWE TO..."

"The only thing some people can achieve on their own is dandruff."
—E. C. McKenzie

West Point humor can be funny, quirky, and sometimes a little off the wall, too. After all, you can't be too serious at a place where seriousness is taken pretty seriously! Humor was a release. When I was a cadet, I had an instructor (Major Schraeder, as I recall - great guy!) who really thought it was even a little sadistic. He was not a West Point graduate, which was unusual in those days. He referred to it simply as Whiskey Papa Hotel (using the army phonetic alphabet for WPH - West Point Humor). He got the biggest charge out of it. He once asked a cadet to describe the funniest thing that had happened to him at West Point. The cadet started giggling and described something really bad that had happened to his roommate. Major Schraeder was almost speechless in total dismay at what the cadet found to be funny.

A good example of Whiskey Papa Hotel is one of the little "funny" traditions at West Point. It occurs at the end of the first summer detail. The upper class squad leaders who have trained the plebes for the first month, make the plebes in their squad say the following, "Sir, all I am or ever hope to be I owe to my first detail squad leader, Mr. Williams" (in my case). The theory is that no matter how famous you become at West Point, or what you do afterwards, it is all because of the great leadership by the first detail squad leader. What a lark! Of course, that's what most plebes were asked(?) to say. Then there were some others, like me, who hadn't done too well during that first summer detail. We were requested(?) to put it this way, "Sir, all I am or ever hope to be I owe to my first detail squad leader who wishes to remain anonymous." The first detail squad leader didn't want to receive any credit, or lack thereof, for the performance of this character. Funny West Point humor? Maybe. Unless, of course, you're the plebe who they're laughing at. Then it was downright degrading. Of course, I tended to be a bit too sensitive anyway.

Humor aside, are there people in your life to whom you owe a lot? Some people who have guided you? Or advised you? Or served as mentors to you? Maybe it was a favorite teacher or a particular coach who positively impacted your life. Maybe it was even someone you weren't close to, but rather someone who expected a lot from you and demanded your best effort. Or it could have been an aunt or uncle who just loved the dickens out of you and treated you nicely when you were a kid. Probably it was someone who built your self-esteem and gave you confidence. Or challenged you to go into something you would have never even considered. Or even made you perform beyond your own expectations. The person was bound to be a nurturer. I know I've had my share. Not long ago I took the time to write them and thank them for the positive influence they've had on me. It was a great experience. You'll have the opportunity to read about them in the dedicated chapters in this book. I mention this for two reasons. First, I would encourage you to **take the time to let the positive people in your life know what they have meant to you.** You never know when it will be too late to thank them. Second, who are <u>you</u> nurturing? Who are <u>you</u> mentoring? How many people will want to write to <u>you</u> some day to say, "Thanks for being there for me?" **Helping people doesn't happen accidentally, but intentionally.** It happens by caring for people and looking for opportunities.

Richard Dreyfuss played a teacher, Mr. Holland, in the movie "Mr. Holland's Opus". It's an excellent movie. Mr. Holland influenced many students as a high school music teacher. He met the kids on their level and built them up one at a time. Always the encourager, he was demanding and yet had a huge amount of empathy. He related to his students on their terms. He gave up his early goal in life to write music because he fell in love with teaching children. He had a gift for music and he could impart it to his students and raise their level of expectation of themselves. He taught them not only about music, but about life. What a gift! Many of his students later in life, took the opportunity to honor him and thank him for his positive influence.

As a successful salesperson, you too have a lot to give. **Don't hold back, share your gifts with others.** When you do, then perhaps some day you'll have someone say to you, "All I am or ever hope to be I owe to _____ (fill in your name here)." What an honor!

Chapter 3

ON BEING AGGRESSIVE

"People are always blaming their circumstances for what they are. I don't believe in circumstances. The people who get on in this world are the people who get up and look for the circumstances they want, and if they can't find them, make them."

— George Bernard Shaw

A few years back I remember hearing a speaker make the following statement, "Don't wait till your ship comes in—swim out to it." It caught my fancy! It's very good advice. Don't be passive and let things happen to you. **Make things happen! Live your life intentionally!** That's what makes most sales positions so unique and so extraordinary. Most of the time you have an opportunity to do just that—make things happen. You don't have to sit around and wait for business to come to you. In fact, in most sales positions you can't. If you do, you're dead in the water. **Sales people are paid handsomely if they get out and do what they do best—sell.** It's an active business rather than a passive business. You can take charge of your life and control your own destiny. Look around you and see how many "jobs" there are that give that same amount of control. Not many. Sales positions are unique. If you are paid on a commission basis, then you get paid exactly what you deserve to get paid—not a penny more nor a penny less. And usually in a commission sales position there are no prejudices. You're going to get paid the same amount any other person would have received if they had sold exactly the same amount. That's great!

What kind of swimmer are you? Are you swimming in life by dog paddling and simply treading water? Not much excitement in that, is there? Are you doing the side stroke with as little effort as possible? That's Okay, I guess, if you're on schedule for a challenging goal. Or are you doing the freestyle and going as hard and as fast as you can? Which one will enable you to reach your ship first? **Live your life intentionally and on purpose. Be aggressive!**

Swim out to your ship. There will be variables that will be beyond your control. The temperature of the water might not be ideal. The waves may be a little higher than you anticipated. The current may be working against you. You just need to shove those things aside and **concentrate and focus on your goal—the ship.** Don't let the variables which you have no control over set you adrift. The economy will continue to be cyclic. Interest rates will rise and fall. Inflation may again become an important factor. There are also unique variables in your particular sales area that have the potential of becoming problems (credit approval, underwriting, inventory control, etc.). No matter! Remember the gun is up and life is not a dress rehearsal. Go for it! Be aggressive! Success is not for the faint of heart. **Don't wait till your ship comes in—swim out to it. And swim hard!**

Chapter 4

TRUST—THE KEY INGREDIENT

"An Emotional Bank Account is a symbol of trust that's been built up in a relationship. If I made deposits into someone's emotional bank account it builds up a reserve and the trust towards me becomes higher."
— Steven Covey

If you are a salesperson (and who isn't?) then you know that you have to sell yourself first before people will buy anything from you. People must first learn to trust you. In other words **you must first develop the relationship before you can begin to make specific product recommendations**. You do this by building rapport with people. Rapport starts when you make a good first impression. The initial seconds are critical with new prospects. Some salespeople claim they can tell whether they're going to sell or not during the first two minutes of an interview. You "connect" with people when you are able to find some common interests and bonds. This helps to reduce the initial relationship tension so that people can relax and not be threatened by your presence. It's attempting to get things off on the right foot. It means making a nice appearance. It also means looking professional in every sense of the word. It means treating people as they would want to be treated. If you can pull that off, you've established a relationship built on trust, the key ingredient.

You need to make the initial contact with every prospect a positive one. What a challenge! How do you do it? You need to keep in mind every aspect of propriety. Are you dressed like a professional? Do your manners speak volumes about the type of person you are? Do you use proper grammar? Are your social graces refined so that you feel comfortable in front of any prospect?

The next area that needs to be addressed is your own competence. **Your prospects are probably wondering what your credentials are and why they should consider doing business with you.** By offering some information about yourself and demonstrating to them your knowledge, your training, experience, and preparation to serve them professionally, they should develop confidence in you. Hopefully, they will come to the conclusion that you are the type of person with whom they would like to do business.

The last obstacle you need to address concerns the sales process itself. Prospects most likely are wondering things like:

"What is this process going to be like?"

"I wonder how he/she is going to treat me?"

"Will this salesperson be like the last one who sold me something and then I never saw her again?"

"Is this going to be another pushy, high pressure sales interview?"

These are all legitimate questions based on your prospects' prior experience with salespeople. What a neat opportunity to demonstrate just how different you are! **If you can prove to people that you will not pressure them and explain to them that you see your role as a "trusted advisor" rather than a "salesperson", then you will have gained your prospect's trust.**

Here are some specific things you can do to establish a relationship built on trust:

1. **Make sure you're in the right frame of mind when you meet the prospect.** Leave all problems back at the office. Act the way you want to feel and pretty soon you'll feel the way you act. Be enthusiastic about your work—always genuine and sincere. Express happiness in as many ways as possible. Be a friend.

2. **Remember that people will always buy for their reasons, not yours.** Try to figure out what those reasons are. What motivates them? Ask questions and do a lot of listening. You'll be surprised to find out how many people think you're a great person when they've done most of the talking.

3. **Get them in a "glad" state of mind.** Mad, sad or scared prospects will probably not buy from you.

4. **Help them like themselves more and they'll love you.** Find ways to genuinely compliment them. Nurture them, encourage them and be "the wind beneath their wings". And, of course, always make sure it's sincere and genuine.

5. **Be aware of the actual physical things you can do to help build trust:**

   A. Smile sincerely (it starts with your eyes);
   B. Keep a relaxed, open stance;
   C. Lean slightly toward the prospect;
   D. Maintain good eye contact (builds confidence and trust);
   E. Use the person's and spouse's name;
   F. Subtly mirror the prospect's behavior (rate of speech, tone, loudness, etc.);
   G. Use humor when and where appropriate.

You're probably very good at building relationships, but it never hurts to review some practical things. **Remember, people want and need to trust you before they'll open up and tell you what they want.** Don't say, "Trust me!". Demonstrate why they can and should trust you and it will be a thousand times more effective. Trust me on that one!

THIS CHAPTER IS DEDICATED TO

JOHN MCCAULEY

John McCauley changed my life. He gave me an opportunity to play football at the college level and I'll never forget him for that. John was in his first year of coaching football at West Point in the fall of 1967. I started out that season as a member of the fifth team defensive backfield. Most schools don't even have that many strings! But John must have seen something in me that most other coaches had not and I kept moving up. Finally, he put me on the first team to try to get the ones he really thought belonged there to work harder and make them a little angry. That was all the chance I needed. I started every game for him that year despite being the second slowest player on the defensive team. (I could beat Jim Bevans, a linebacker we called "snowshoes", barely!). John McCauley is a perfectionist extraordinaire! He never let a player get by with anything! If we did something wrong John spotted it and corrected it instantaneously. Some of the players thought he was too critical. I thought he walked on water. When John spoke I listened. When John spoke I learned because John was a great fundamentals coach. Of all the coaches I've been around, I think he got the most mileage out of the players he was coaching.

John, you were the best coach I ever had. Thank you for demanding my best. While I don't miss the twenty 40's you used to make us run (20 forty yard sprints for conditioning), I do miss your tutelage, your New England accent, and your friendship! Thank you for your fanatical perfectionism. Thank you for your attention to detail. Thank you for having high expectations. Thank you for hating to lose. Thank you for making me demand of myself my very best effort-every time. It has been my privilege to know you not only as a coach, but to know you as a friend. Your strong religious convictions, your loving family culture, your wit and sense of humor and your tremendous work ethic have influenced me far beyond your imagination. Thanks, John, for your positive influence and nurturing; but mainly thank you for giving me my chance. It's made all the difference in the world in my life. John, I love you!

Dick

Chapter 5

CONFIDENCE

"When I went duck hunting with Bear Bryant, he shot at one but it kept flying. 'John,' he said, 'there flies a dead duck.' Now that's confidence."
— John McKay

Confidence. It's an attitude. It's a belief in yourself. It's thinking you can do the job. It's feeling capable. It's a fantastic feeling too! No more cowardice sensations, or uneasiness, or anxiety—just faith in yourself to do it.

While confidence may be easy to describe, it is almost impossible to teach. Confidence simply must be earned. When I coached football at West Point one of the hardest things to do was to impart confidence in the players. They had talent. They had good skills. They were knowledgeable. The cadets were very coachable kids who would listen and learn. **Confidence, however, must be earned, not learned!** You simply cannot give it to someone.

At the beginning of the football season of my junior year at West Point, I was the fifth team defensive halfback. Did you ever realize they had a depth chart that long?! When we opened up the season six weeks later, I was the starting defensive halfback. What happened in those six weeks? Did my skills and abilities change? Sure, a little. But I didn't get any faster and there certainly wasn't a drastic difference in my skill level. What changed was my attitude. I gained confidence. The only variable that could change that drastically in six weeks was my confidence. Once I was put on the first team, no one was going to move me out of there. What a great lesson to learn first hand. The coaches may have seen my potential, but as the fifth team defensive back I did not yet realize that I could compete at that level. Once I earned the right to be up there, however, I was a different athlete. I earned the position through hard work and I retained the position through a confident attitude and a desire to succeed.

How are you doing in the confidence department? My experience as a sales manager indicates to me that there are a lot of very good people in sales. Unfortunately, many of them don't see themselves as being successful. As a result, they do not project themselves as being confident. **Somehow that lack of confidence is consciously or subconsciously conveyed to the buyer and derails many sales opportunities.**

Confidence is conveyed to people in many different ways. Perhaps it's in a person's gait. Maybe it's their firm handshake. Perhaps it's their smile and easy way they treat people. Possibly it's the silence they allow before answering people in an interview. Most likely, it's all of the above and many other little things which tip off the buyer that they're dealing with a real professional. Confident people aren't difficult to spot. They're the one's who are leading their company in sales. They're the one's who are willing to risk a little more because they know they're knowledgeable, trustworthy, and can handle just about anything thrown their way.

Confidence. Easy to describe; difficult to attain. **Most of us have to earn it simply through perseverance, hard work, and experiencing success.** Each failure is a learning experience and simply one step closer to the day when we have that feeling that everything is going to work out just fine. Confidence? Don't treat it lightly. It's one of the most under-rated characteristics of most successful people. It's a mental attitude that says, "I'm a winner! There's nothing that I can't accomplish through hard work and persistence." Walk tall; self-assured; confident. People will begin to react differently to you.

Chapter 6

GUARANTEED STAGNATION

"Stagnant water loses its purity and in cold weather becomes frozen; even so does inaction sap the vigor of the mind."

—Leonardo da Vinci

It's easy to become complacent. **Stagnation can set in if we're not careful.** We've all gotten into ruts before. We like to stay in our "comfort zone," don't we? We lose our enthusiasm and zest for what we're doing if we're not careful. Here are some deadly signs that will most certainly lead to stagnation. If you've said or thought any of these recently, BEWARE!

1. We're not ready for that!

2. We're doing alright without it!

3. That will never work!

4. I tried that once before!

5. "My people" wouldn't go for that!

6. We've never done it that way before!

7. That's just not me!

8. That's just not my market!

9. That worked for a while, so I stopped doing it!

10. I'm not comfortable with that!

Listen to your self talk. **Be careful what you're thinking. You're just liable to get it!** Be open and receptive to new ideas. The world around us is rapidly changing. Be prepared to take advantage of that. Be proactive. Get out of a defensive posture. Be willing to risk more. **Learning and being willing to risk are going to be the tickets to success in the future.** Fail your way to success by being open and willing to try new things. By all means get out of your comfort zone. Good luck and keep trying.

Chapter 7

"TODAY I BEGIN A NEW LIFE"*

*"The best verse hasn't been rhymed yet,
the best house hasn't been planned,
the highest peak hasn't been climbed yet,
the mightiest rivers aren't spanned;
Don't worry and fret, faint-hearted,
the chances have just begun
for the best jobs haven't been started,
the best work hasn't been done."*
—Berton Braley

"Today I begin a new life!" Yesterday is over. Last week's events have come and gone, and last month is ancient history. In a way that's too bad if they were good ones; fortunate if they were bummers and ones you'd just as soon forget. Regardless of what kind of day, week or month it's been, it was at the very least, a learning experience. "Today I begin a new life." **Learn from your experience**. If it was a good one; build on it. If it was a bad experience don't repeat it. It's time to start over, form good habits, start fresh, and begin anew.

Remember the magic slates you played with as a kid? I liked them! You were able to start over and erase what was on the slate. Wipe things out. Get a fresh start. No liabilities. No white-out necessary. "Today I begin a new life." In the movie, "City Slickers" (my all-time favorite), they called it a "do over". Life is a "do over". Every day you have an opportunity to start over. You hold your destiny in your own hands.

Not satisfied with yesterday's performance or results? No problem. Today you can try it again and get it right this time. Why? Because "Today I begin a new life"!

Today you start the first day of the rest of your life. What kind of day will it be? Will it bring fulfillment? Accomplishment? Productivity? New breakthroughs? You make the call. It's all in your hands. You determine its success or failure. You have the ability to control your destiny. "Today I begin a new life!" Wow! What an opportunity! You'll never have this day again. **Today you have an opporunity to excel and to begin a new life.** Shed your old skin. Don't settle for anything less than your best shot. Dump the old way of thinking. Challenge the way you do everything! Be born again and begin a new life. You are God's most amazing creation—made in His own image. You are designed for success and engineered for greatness. Don't settle for your second best effort. Go for it! Don't wallow in negative thinking. Don't mire in the disgust of self-pity or join in the notions of those who don't aspire to succeed like you do. Heed not the reasons or excuses others give for their failures or shortcomings. **Listen to your own self-talk and positive affirmations.** Listen to the advice of one of the wisest of all men, King Solomon himself, "A joyful heart makes a cheerful face, but with a heartache comes depression... Every day is a terrible day for a miserable person, but a cheerful heart has a continual feast" (Prov. 15:13,15). Sage advice! Make today a continual feast! Why choose to be miserable? **Choose instead to be cheerful and positive!** Put a song in your heart. It will change your outlook on life!

"Today I begin a new life." Wow, what possibilities! For me, life will never be the same as B.C. (before cancer). Cancer has a way of getting your attention. It was a "wake-up call" you couldn't sleep through! From now on every moment is precious and every day is a gift. My life began anew. No more old habits. No more time for being "down" or moody, or settling for anything less than my best effort, or taking things for granted. Today, a new beginning. A clean slate. A "do-over". The rest of your life starts now, today. What can you do differently? Here are three suggestions:

1. **Do more of the things that failures won't do.**
2. **Try to stay out of your comfort zone for longer periods of time.**
3. **No matter what happens: be cheerful!**

If you can master these three things it will not only help you accomplish more of your goals but it will greatly improve the quality of your life. "Today I begin a new life!" Good luck!

* The title of the Scroll Marked I from Og Mandino's classic best seller *The Greatest Salesman in the World*, Lifetime Books Publisher

Chapter 8

FOCUS

"A fanatic is one who can't change his mind and won't change the subject."
—Winston Churchill

Have you been to a race track recently? Have you noticed that the horses wear blinders? Blinders force the horses to focus straight ahead and not become distracted by anything on either side of them during the race. This practice makes great sense because the only reason the horse is on the track is to run straight toward the finish line and win the race.

We can learn a great lesson from this. We're all, to a certain extent, in a race. It may not be exactly the same race for each of us, but it's a race nonetheless. Some of us are running for survival. Some of us are running for recognition. Some of us are running for financial rewards. Others still are running for success by other definitions. During this "race", **it is very easy to get distracted to the point where we have lost our focus and lost sight of our goal.** The possibilities for distractions in a sales career are almost too numerous to mention. You know them better than I do. The distractions can slow our pace, divert us from our path or even stop us in our tracks.

Distractions! They sap your strength and energy. They slow you down. They destroy your momentum. They're costly no matter how you look at them. What they exhaust is your emotional energy. Everyone has a limited amount of emotional energy to run their race. By allowing distractions, this energy is siphoned off and we start to sputter.

How can we put blinders on in our race? The first thing to do is **recognize the things in our race that are distractions to us.** If we can recognize them for what they are then we can start to eliminate them or at least minimize them.

The second thing is to be sure we know where the finish line is. **Having written goals which are constantly in front of us helps us determine exactly where we are headed.** It's easier to stay focused when we are obsessed with winning and achieving a specific goal.

The third thing is to be sure **we take time to plan our race.** It's a lot easier to stay focused and keep the blinders on if we know exactly how we're going to get there. Many people seem to live life like this: ready, fire, aim! It's critical to take time to plan. **Live your life intentionally!**

Lastly, **periodic reviews** will help to evaluate how we are doing and to recognize when we have been blindsided by diversions. These reviews should help us to get back on course, focus on the finish line and keep our emotional energy full.

We can learn a lot from the horses in a race. **They stay focused because they are not easily distracted** by all the little things that are going on around them. We're much more intelligent than horses are, yet it's not a bad idea to put on blinders in our own race. Remember, the prize doesn't always go to the swiftest but to the one who crosses the finish line first. Oftentimes the one with the blinders on runs the straightest.

Chapter 9

LEARNED OPTIMISM

"Keep your face to the sunshine . . . and you cannot see the shadows."
—Helen Keller

I tend to be optimistic. I try to look for the silver lining in every cloud. I look for the rainbows after a shower and gratefully remember God's promise. I never spend much time reading the newspaper—too negative. Sometimes I get criticized for being too much like Pollyanna. That's okay with me. To me, it beats the alternative. Today we are bombarded by every media imaginable with **nothing** but criticism, cynicism, negativism and other "ism's" I can't even comprehend. It can get to you if you let it. **Life's too short to spend so much time in negative thinking.** It occurs to me that sooner or later some of the doomsdayers will be right simply because they've been predicting negative things for so long. It's like the economic forecasters—they've correctly predicted 18 of the last 2 recessions. No matter how bad a situation is, I remember the promise of Romans 8:28, that "...all things work together for the good of those who love God." While there are things that happen which are not pleasant (cancer for me) and events which occur that are downright demoralizing, there is almost always something positive that can happen as a result of those situations. **Problems, in effect, present us with opportunities.** If you examine the great entrepreneurial explosion in this country which has occurred in the last twenty years, it can be almost entirely attributed to the downsizing of our corporations and the technological advancements which caused people to be replaced by machines. Men and women of all ages who no longer had a job put their ingenuity to work and came up with ideas which created jobs. They simply turned their negative situation into a positive one. And the world has vastly improved on account of it. Time and again throughout history the same phenomena occurs—**when people are faced with adversity, or a seemingly insurmountable problem, they turn it into an opportunity and a positive situation.**

The title of this chapter is also the title of a book written by Dr. Martin E.P. Seligman (*Learned Optimism*). By its title the author suggests that optimism can, in fact, be learned. In other words, we can all improve our outlook no matter how optimistic or pessimistic we are naturally. I'd like to make some suggestions along those lines myself:

1. **Make sure that your attitude reflects what you want to accomplish.** Be positive! Block out negative thoughts —it's wasted energy. People in positions similar to yours refuse to let "things" stand in their way. They refuse the excuses that seem to warrant not making their goal, and they make their goal anyway. They rise above any amount of negative things thrown in their path and they succeed anyway. Hooray for them!

2. **Make certain that you're not "fueling" the notion that things are bad.** Every time you talk about how bad things are, you are adding to the notion and fulfilling your own prophecy. Even in the best of times, it's easy to be negative. And even in the worst of times it's possible to be positive.

Choose to be positive and optimistic. Remember, every time you say something negative you are subconsciously reinforcing that negative thought yourself. Don't permit it!

3. In a word (or two) **be persistent.** Through good times and bad, persistence will help make you successful. By being persistent, something good will happen and, all of a sudden, you pick up some momentum.

4. Focus on other people's needs. **Nothing is more persuasive in selling than a genuine desire to help people.** When people recognize that you are sincerely interested in helping them, they will most likely want to do business with you. If not now, then sometime down the road (read number three again to be sure you get that "down the road" business). What does this one have to do with optimism? Well, it's pretty hard to be "down" when you're concentrating on other people and helping them solve their problems. All of a sudden, with a sale or two, you're back on top of the world and it's hard to be pessimistic when you're doing well.

So there you have it —an easy four step process. You know better! At times it's tougher than normal to be optimistic. **But it is always a choice! Choose to be optimistic!**

Chapter 10

INTERVIEW TECHNIQUE #1 BUILDING TRUST

Your first contact with prospects needs to be a positive one. It shouldn't be tense and stressful. Some successful salespeople say they know in the first two minutes whether they're going to ultimately make a sale or not. **That means first impressions are paramount!** While initial relationship tension is usually high, you can reduce it so that it can be constructive and positive. Take some time to warm-up your prospects a little before getting right down to business. Try to connect with them by finding common interests or a common ground. You can do that by getting them to talk. Just as a carpenter's tools are saws and hammers, a salesperson's tools are questions. By asking good questions you can engage your prospects and get them to open up a little. Next, you want to earn the right to address several issues that are probably going through your prospects' minds. How do you do that? You do it by demonstrating empathy to your prospects. Imagine yourself being the prospect. What questions would be going through your mind?

"I don't know this person from Adam. I wonder if I can trust him?"
"I wonder how she's going to treat me?"
"I remember that last salesperson. Does this one know what he's talking about?"
"Is she going to high pressure me?"
"What's the sales process going to be like?"

"Is she going to ask me to buy today?"
"I wonder if this company is any good?"

If you can effectively address these main issues, you will have launched a successful relationship. In a nutshell, **it's building trust.** People need to be able to trust you before they will part with their money no matter how good your product is. **You have to "sell yourself" to your prospects before you even talk about your company or your prospects' needs.** The key technique here is **positioning**. You must earn the right to answer the questions. You can demonstrate empathy by telling your prospects exactly how you'd feel if you were them. A simple statement like, "If I were you, here's what I'd be wondering . . ." and then verbalize some of the questions listed above. Now you have earned the right to address those questions or concerns and answer them.

Remember, you're trying to establish long term relationships with your prospects. **The best way to do that is to connect with them.** Give them reasons to trust you. **Demonstrate empathy for how they are probably feeling by positioning, so that you can earn the right to address those feelings or concerns.** Nothing will give you a better feeling about this first interview than building trust and earning their confidence. The whole sales process starts with this first step. Without it you won't get much further. **Build trust and get your initial contact off to a great start.**

Chapter 11

TOTAL INTEGRITY

"Some things that I have strictly adhered to are: to have integrity, to never deceive anybody, to have my word good. Under no circumstances deviate from that."
— Conrad Hilton

Mark Twain once said, "Always do right. This will surprise some people and astonish the rest." Cute humor? Maybe, but not when your business and professional life are totally based on trust and integrity. **Doing the right thing must be a constant.** It must not only be your "modus operandi" (way of operating), but also your "modus vivendi" (way of living). People can spot a phony. People can also discern between a salesperson who is in it for the sale and a person who cares about them and does what is right.

We have adopted a philosophy in our insurance agency which addresses this very issue of integrity. Here are some of the things we espouse:

> We believe that character is what you do when you think no one is looking.
> We believe in order for us to win, our clients must win first.
> We believe our clients want agents of trust and integrity—not just policies.
> We believe the professional agent will be honest and ethically above reproach.
> We believe in treating our clients as we would like to be treated.

We believe in Solomon's advice: "Be kind and honest and you will live a long life; others will respect you and treat you fairly." (Prov. 21:21)

There's an old Latin expression you've heard many times, **"Caveat emptor"** (let the buyer beware). **It has absolutely no place in business today. We're beyond that.** Today our customers expect more than ever before and they deserve more than ever before. When our customers buy something from us there should be no surprises. **They deserve to know exactly what they're getting.**

In 1932 a Chicago Rotarian was asked to save a company from bankruptcy. He decided to strengthen its moral character. He came up with four key questions to establish a code of ethics for their salespeople. This code has become known as the Four-Way Test:

Is it the truth?

Is it fair to all concerned?

Will it build good-will and better friendships?

Will it be beneficial to all concerned?

These are excellent questions to ask ourselves in all business situations. If there is any doubt about the answer to any one of the four questions, then chances are you should probably back off. Every business transaction should be done with the long term best interest of your customers in mind.

Integrity is not a sometimes thing. It is an always thing! You should not adopt ethics because that leads to financial success; rather, you should always do what is right because that's the right thing to do. Most people today as adults know right from wrong. **The key is getting in the habit of doing what is right 100% of the time.** There should be only one position in regard to integrity—total and absolute.

Chapter 12

CARPE DIEM

"Opportunity rarely knocks on your door. Knock rather on opportunity's door if you ardently wish to enter."
— B. C. Forbes

One of the more talented actors of our time is Robin Williams. His hit movie "Mrs. Doubtfire" brings a smile to my face when I think of some of the scenes. As Mork in the hit TV show "Mork and Mindy", he was sensational. If you've ever seen him as a guest on the David Letterman Show or a similar program, you know he's really bonkers. Certainly he qualifies as a great actor and an absolute loony. He's quick witted, spontaneous, ad-libs with the best of them, and probably performs best as a comic with little script and lots of leeway. Just wind him up and let him go. My favorite movie with him, however, is in a very serious role as a new professor at a very exclusive prep school in "Dead Poet's Society". It's an excellent movie and a real thought provoker. He challenges his young prodigies with the Latin term **Carpe diem—seize the day.** What excellent advice! The advice is applicable to many occupations and situations, but probably none more fitting than sales. Your business gives you the opportunity to carpe diem. You have the ability to:

"Take the bull by the horn";

"Call your own shots";

"Determine your own destiny";

"Make your own breaks";

"Live your life intentionally";

"Be the master of your fate";

"Make things happen";

"Take charge of your life."

Essentially, your whole business is in your own hands. That gives you the opportunity and the challenge to plan and then do. It also just happens to be the main reason why many people fail in a sales career. **They don't carpe diem. They think they can carpe diem next week.** They kid themselves into believing they're working hard when, in fact, they're spending way too much time at their desks. **They spend far too much time on the planning side of the equation and precious little on the doing side.** They get comfortable. They lose their competitiveness. They get out of their groove. They lose momentum. They let a one week training school they attend turn into a three weeks out of production syndrome. They start getting comfortable, letting things happen to them rather than making things happen. They tend to forget their first year in the business when they didn't receive one phone call from someone who wanted a product or service—they had to solicit them all. So they don't carpe diem. They think there's plenty of time in the day so there's no sense, "rushing into anything this early". They like the idea of improving the technology they use, but they don't want to carpe diem by learning more about it and using it to their advantage. Carpe diem means setting goals, but that means risk and possibly failing. **Carpe diem also means being held accountable for activity and sales results.**

In "Dead Poet's Society", Robin Williams challenges his students to "Go For It!" Don't dangle your toes in the water—dive in! Don't be afraid of failure and not risk. Risk! Seize the day! **Give the business you're in your absolute best shot.** Don't worry about other people's expectations of you. Demand it of yourself! Hold yourself accountable for a high activity level. Remember that, generally speaking, **no one fails in a selling career because of the people they don't sell. People fail because of the people they don't see!** Carpe diem! I can think of no other business when this saying, carpe diem, will lead more quickly to success than a selling career. Carpe diem! Good advice even if it comes from a wallflower like Robin Williams! **Carpe diem! Today, tomorrow and every day!**

Chapter 13

LEADING BY EXAMPLE

"You can preach a better sermon with your life than with your lips."

— Goldsmith

Could you ever imagine buying a Cadillac from a salesperson who was driving a Lincoln? It sounds ludicrous, doesn't it? I've experienced enough salespeople in my lifetime, however, to tell you it isn't as far fetched as it sounds. Maybe you're selling a product where it would be impossible or impractical to own the product you're selling. That's certainly understandable. Not many people for example, have need of a nuclear power plant. **As salespeople you must 'walk your talk'. You must be willing to own whatever product you're selling.** You should also own it in enough quantity to demonstrate your "belief" in the product. You cannot be like the shoemaker's children who went without shoes. That just doesn't cut it. Or the barber who looks unkempt.

Your customers rely on you to educate them about your products, to advise them with recommendations and to help them decide what to purchase. In order for you to do that you not only have to know an awful lot about your products, but you also need to demonstrate your belief in them as well.

My area of expertise happens to be the financial services industry. It's important for me to own as many of the products my company offers as I can. Then I can have empathy for our customers and advise them how the products work and why I am recommending the product for their particular situation. If I am recommending an insurance product for a child, probably one of the best things I can say is, "This is the exact type of policy that I bought for my children." Wow, instant credibility! If, on the other hand, I was recommending something entirely different, what I in effect would be saying to this parent is, "Don't do as I do, do as I say." If I only owned $100,000 of insurance, it would be pretty difficult for me to ask someone else to buy a $1,000,000 policy, wouldn't it? The point is, we must believe in our products so much that we ourselves purchase them. **In essence, our first sale must be to ourselves.**

In order for you to sell something to someone else you must first be sold on the product yourself. If you are, you should purchase it and own it yourself. Then you can talk first hand about how it feels to own it. One of the best things insurance agents can do is to carry their policies with them (or at least a list of them). They can then show their customers exactly what they have purchased and now own. That's impressive. That builds trust and credibility. That's what leading by example is all about.

How are you doing in this regard? Have everything you need? Anything missing in your portfolio? If you can't afford it now, then at least put it in your plans for the future. **Leading by example is imperative in a selling career.** Make sure all your bases are covered. Demonstrating to your customers that you own the exact same thing you are recommending can be a very good close. Don't kid yourself. People are not stupid. They expect more today than ever before. They expect to be served by someone who truly believes in what they're selling.

When you can demonstrate that belief in a tangible way by telling them you own it too, you've gone a long way toward building a solid long term relationship. **Sell yourself first and lead by example!**

Chapter 14

"NICE GUYS FINISH LAST"

"Good manners and soft words have brought many a difficult thing to pass."

—Aesop

These famous words were once spoken by Leo Durocher at the old Polo Grounds when he was managing the Brooklyn Dodgers during a pennant race in the late 1940's. Leo, "the lip", as he was called back then, was a real scrapper. He was a fierce competitor who hated to lose. He was chatting with sports writers in the dugout prior to a game against the rival New York Giants. As the Giants emerged from their dugout to take their warm ups, Leo quipped, "Take a look at them. All nice guys. They'll finish last. Nice guys finish last."

Don't believe it for a second! You don't have to be rude, cocky, arrogant and ruthless today in order to succeed. Despite the arrogance and insolent behavior of many pro athletes today, you don't have to emulate that kind of behavior in order to be successful. It seems today the more abrasive and disrespectful pro athletes are, the more attention and adulation they receive. Too bad! They're negatively influencing many young people today. They're teaching that breaking the rules, winning at all costs and total disregard for authority is Okay. They have helped create an "in your face" mentality that thrives on confrontation, defiance, and contemptuous disregard for authority. Most of them are failures as modern role models.

You don't have to demonstrate rudeness and belligerent behavior to be a successful salesperson today. As a matter of fact, just the opposite is true. **People love to do business with someone they respect, trust and admire.** They would prefer to do business with a friend, frankly, than simply an acquaintance. To be a friend you have to demonstrate empathy, caring and a commitment to always do what is right. You have to, at all times, put your customer's needs above your needs. **You have to show compassion, understanding and demonstrate trust.** You have to be a good listener in order to figure out how to help your customer. Here are some other "sure-fire" things to do in order to qualify as a truly "nice guy":

- **Smile sincerely when meeting your customers;**
- Listen and allow your customers to talk freely and openly;
- **Give positive feedback whenever possible (this will encourage even more dialogue);**
- Be careful about manipulating. It can be viewed negatively even when it's properly motivated;
- Develop the habit of maintaining good eye contact;
- Go out of your way to be pleasant, warm and friendly;
- **Be "customer conscious" at all times. Look for ways to remember customers in special ways;**
- Clip and send articles and information that will be helpful to your customers. It doesn't have to be business related either;
- Always send a "thank you" note after every meeting;
- Call customers up without trying to do business;

- Take an interest in their families and their outside activities;
- Find out what their most proud of—then ask about it periodically.
- **Treat them royally without expecting anything in return.**
- Conduct yourself professionally and ethically and model servitude.
- **Answer all questions thoroughly, patiently and non-judgmentally.**

If you do half of these things exceptionally well, the sky's the limit! Do nice guys finish last? Sometimes perhaps. But probably never because they're nice guys!! Chances are pretty good, as a matter of fact, that the nicer they are, the better relationships they've established. **If given a choice, people would generally rather do business with someone they like and trust—a friend—than with someone they really don't know very well.**

"Nice guys finish last" is about as accurate as saying, "You should treat all people the same." Just as sure as different folks require different strokes, nice guys don't finish last. **In relationships, "nice guys" will always be near the top.** If you're perceived as a "nice guy", chances are your customers trust and respect you and you're well on your way to a winning long-term relationship.

Chapter 15

HEALTH AND FITNESS

"As a nation we are dedicated to keeping physically fit —and parking as close to the stadium as possible."
—Bill Vaughan

America has been going through a fitness revolution in the past decade. The fitness craze, while it has slowed down, has not come to a screeching halt. Yet, despite the rush to join health clubs, have your own personal trainer, and order the newest fitness apparatus for use in the convenience of your own home, we as Americans have not greatly improved our health. Young people are experiencing some of the lowest scores in physical aptitude tests in years and the increase in sedentary lifestyle among the youth of our country is downright alarming. The term "couch potato," which was non-existent twenty years ago, now describes a growing percentage of our young people.

Why are we having problems? The problems have grown to epidemic proportions for any number of reasons. Video games and computer communications have become the "exercise" of choice for many younger Americans. Hour after hour of sitting in front of a computer or video game makes for a larger percentage of body fat and leaves little time for physical fitness. Throw in America's passion for home rental video movies (one of the real growth markets of the last 10 years) and it's easy to understand the dilemma. Too much sitting!

The problem is compounded by the American diet. We consume way too much red meat and animal fat, and cancer will very shortly pass heart disease as the number one killer in

America. Not exactly a great picture, is it? As our society has become almost preoccupied with fast food, quick meals and instant solutions, we have not exercised discretion in deciding what food we put into our bodies. When people go to the grocery store today, most often they're looking for solutions not ingredients. They're looking for complete meals rather than the natural essentials to prepare a meal. The preservatives and other unnatural ingredients in these "pre-fab" meals only add to the unhealthiness of our situation. **Since the results of such action are almost always deferred, most Americans have not yet had their day of reckoning.** That's most unfortunate because we have been lulled into a false sense of security. We have not yet had to fess up to years of bodily abuse. The younger generation which grew up on fast food, pizza and microwaveable instant meals, may yet feel the consequences of this lifestyle most of all.

The last factor in the health equation, is the pace of life today and the pressures involved in our lifestyle. In business we are asked to do more than ever before. When companies downsized they didn't change the amount of work performed, they simply heaped it on fewer workers. In America costs have come down on many items in an attempt to be competitive with products prepared in foreign countries by workers whose conditions are deplorable and whose wages are paltry. The American corporation has become more productive, but sometimes at the expense of the American worker. The term "burn-out" is a modern word probably without definition a generation ago. The rapidity of change and having to cope with it, has also added its burden to the list of factors. The sandwich generation trying to cope with raising children as well as caring for parents, is also a sobering reality of life and a source of stress for many people. **Stress today is a major problem**. Wow! That's a lot to handle.

So far the medical profession has pretty much chosen to engage in symptom management while ignoring preventative programs. It is my view that this will change drastically in the years to come as nutritionists and others involved in preventative medicine are finally heard by the American people. It cannot come quickly enough. Despite all this, people are living longer. We cannot dispute that. Until we change the lifestyle issues mentioned above, however, we will continue to find more and more people being treated for cancer and heart disease rather than preventing these things in the first place.

What does this have to do with salespeople? Well, our lifestyle fits the description of just about everything mentioned above. Then, when you add the pressure of not getting paid until you sell something, it's easy to see just how stressful our lives can be. What can we do about it? The solution is not a simple one. You can't just take a pill and be done with it. It just doesn't work that way. **You have to be willing to take total responsibility for your health and fitness.** In order to <u>do</u> your best you have to <u>be</u> at your best. **It is your responsibility to be informed and knowledgeable about nutrition and health issues.** Your every day life should also include some sort of fitness program. Dr. Kenneth Cooper, who has been described as the man who pioneered the fitness movement, suggests some form of aerobic exercise for a minimum of 30 minutes three times a week. Walking, jogging, aerobics, racquetball, swimming and biking are but a few of the aerobic options available today (billiards and chess rank 78th and 79th). By working out regularly you should be able to bring your heart rate to between 50 to 60 beats per minute which is excellent.

Decreasing your caloric intake is no longer enough to satisfy the diet side of the equation. **You must learn what foods are good for you and what foods should be avoided.** It's not as hard as you might think. An obvious over-simplification is that fruit and vegetables and other foods with fiber are good for you, while red meat and other foods with high fat content are not. It is certainly beyond the scope of this chapter to recommend a diet and a physical fitness program, but rather to **emphasize the need for you to develop one yourself.**

What are the benefits of being healthy and physically fit? High self-esteem—feeling good about the way you look and the way you feel. Greater energy for work and play and family time. Dr. Cooper himself summed it up pretty well when he said, **"There are a number of benefits such as greater enthusiasm, better energy levels, increased confidence and improved attitudes."** While it's not easy to always be health conscious and fitness oriented, in the long run it will be well worth the effort.

Chapter 16

LISTENING

"The courage to speak must be matched by the wisdom to listen."

— Author Unknown

Your brain can comprehend about 1,000 words per minute, while your mouth can speak an average of about 150 words per minute. What's wrong with this picture? That presents a real problem to the listener, because your brain has an awful lot of idle time. **You must work hard at becoming an empathetic, active listener.** Empathetic active listening means trying to understand the speaker from his or her perspective. To be a great listener, you also need to refrain from judging what the speaker is saying prematurely. That's an error which happens all the time. The speaker is only halfway through a sentence when the listener cuts off the speaker and finishes the sentence for her. Ouch! That may work Okay (not really!) with good friends, but it will almost never work in a selling situation. **Listening skills are vital in selling situations because as the seller, you need to learn what is important to the buyer.** Every time your customer speaks, you are gaining valuable information. If your questions are good ones, the customer will end up telling you exactly what he or she will buy and why.

Here are four other tips to help you become a better listener:

1. **Don't worry about your response while you are listening.** Don't think you have to immediately respond to a comment or question. Focus on the speaker! Silence is golden. Silence after your prospect finishes is excellent. It will allow prospects to say more if they desire and it will also allow you to deliberate over your response. That shows respect for what the prospects had to say.

2. **Ask questions.** Get the speaker to say more. Phrases like, "That's an interesting observation. Why do you feel that way?" or just, "Interesting. Why is that important to you?" These questions should elicit valuable information. They will also buy you some time to mentally prepare your response.

3. **Rephrase what you think you've heard.** This will help confirm what was said or clarify it better for you. That's called a checking question. Here's an example: "So what you're saying is you're not exactly sure if you can afford this new copier right now? Is that correct?" After the answer to this question, you know for sure exactly what was being said. You've also bought some time to formulate a response. In addition the prospect comes away feeling you've really been a good listener. That's valuable.

4. **Remove all distractions if possible.** Ask for the television to be turned off. Avoid anything that will distract you from your prime objective—empathetic listening. Focus on your customer. Have good eye contact and be sure to nod and encourage more from your customer. A forward lean and genuine interest will demonstrate attentiveness and encourage your customer to keep talking.

Listening takes concentration and it's very hard work. The good news is that we can all get better at it. It is certainly a learned skill which can be improved. Don't make the mistake many salespeople do. They think they have to talk a lot to be effective. The exact opposite is probably a lot closer to reality. **Listen and your customers will tell you exactly what you need to hear—what they will most likely buy.** Continue to improve your listening skills and watch your sales soar. Your customers will love it too!

Chapter 17

WHAT YOUR CUSTOMERS REALLY BUY

"A drop of honey catches more flies than a gallon of gall. So with men. If you would win a man to your cause, first convince him that you are his sincere friend. Therein is a drop of honey which catches his heart, which, say what he will, is the high road to his reason."
—Abe Lincoln

What exactly are you "selling"? Sometimes it's not the product you think you are selling, as unusual as this may sound.

- People want security, love, acceptance and success.
- They want someone they can trust to help them.
- They want hope for their goals and their dreams.
- **They want people to listen to them.**
- **They want long term relationships.**
- They want flexibility and choices.
- They want great service.
- **They want to know you care about them.**
- People tend to buy familiar brand names over strange names.
- **They buy convenience in buying and paying.**
- They buy from people who have knowledge.
- They buy from people who can inspire and lead them.
- They buy from people who have positioned themselves professionally.

- They buy from people who have committed themselves to personal growth and development.
- **They buy for their own reasons not your reasons.**
- They buy certainties and guarantees.
- They buy "things" they have read about.
- They buy because of recommendations by other professionals (accountant, attorney etc.).
- **They buy solutions not ingredients.**
- They buy because they believe you care about them.

Don't ever underestimate how important you are in this process. **Before they will ever consider buying a product, they must first be sold on you. Your first "sale" to them, therefore, must be you.** Market yourself in such a way that it instills confidence, trust and a desire to work with you. **Market yourself so the message screams at them, "This person is different!"** Then, if you listen to what they need and want, the rest will be easy.

Chapter 18

A SELF-FULFILLING PROPHECY

"Nothing can stop the man with the right mental attitude from achieving his goal; nothing on earth can help the man with the wrong mental attitude."
—Thomas Jefferson

A whole lot has been written on the subject of positive thinking. Authors who have written and lectured extensively on the subject would read like a "Who's Who" of motivational speakers. One of the premier speakers currently in vogue, Stephen Covey, wrote this in his book *The Seven Habits of Highly Effective People,* "Begin with the end in mind. Visualize your success and it will become reality." I like that.

Billy Crystal just happens to be one of my favorite comedians. I've probably seen his movie, "City Slickers", at least eight times and laugh more each time I see it. It's my favorite all-time movie. Billy Crystal was interviewed by Bob Costas on late night TV some time ago and was asked if, when he was younger, he ever thought he'd be as successful as he is today. It was obvious to me that Bob Costas expected him to say something like, "Not in my wildest dreams did I ever think I'd be this successful." Instead, without hesitation Billy Crystal said, "Absolutely!" He said he can remember as vividly as if it were yesterday, being six years old standing in his bathroom and using his toothbrush as a microphone accepting an Emmy. Wow! That calls not only for a lot of confidence but also a great imagination. **His mind saw success—imagined it— and it became a reality.** Positive thinking. **It was a self-fulfilling prophecy.**

How do you imagine yourself? Your own actions and behaviors are the results of your own images and beliefs. **Mental pictures allow you to develop new traits and new attitudes which will enable you to succeed.** Remember the Vietnam prisoner of war who practiced round after round of golf in his mind while being imprisoned for over seven years? Within one week of his release he shot within one stroke of his previous handicap after not having played the game physically for over seven years. When asked if he was surprised his reply was great, "No, I never missed a putt in prison in seven years!" In his book *Psycho-Cybernetics,* Maxwell Maltz reported that an experiment was conducted with three groups of people. The first group shot basketballs on the first day and their scores were recorded. Then they practiced every day for 20 days. On the 20th day they shot again and their scores were recorded. They improved by 24%. The second group's shots were scored on the first day and the 20th day and they didn't practice in between. Their scores showed no improvement at all. The third group's scores were recorded on the first day. Then they spent 20 minutes a day for the next 20 days imagining shooting and scoring a basket. On the 20th day their scores were again recorded. Their scores had improved by 38%! Just by imagining success they had improved drastically without ever having touched a ball for 20 days.

Imaging is probably the newest training technique in sports today. It's a mental rehearsal. Players of all sports listen to motivational music like the theme from "Rocky" or "Chariots of

Fire" and watch themselves over and over hitting a home run or catching a tough pass, or shooting the winning basket, or sinking that difficult 25 foot putt. They also sit back in comfortable reclining chairs, close their eyes and are talked through a series of successes in their particular sport. They imagine themselves scoring the winning field goal over arch-rival Navy, or hitting the home run that wins the World Series. **They see it in their mind and their mind cannot distinguish between real and imagined.**

If you want to change the way others see you, you must first change the way you see yourself. Walter Doyle Staples, Ph.D., a Canadian Psychologist and author of *Think Like a Winner*, says this, "What you think you are is what you show. Other people see in you what you see in yourself. They accept your estimation of yourself."

Have you ever imagined that perfect interview where you close that million dollar sale? Why not? Do you see yourself succeeding? Do you see yourself coming up front at an Awards Banquet and accepting the award for being the Most Valuable Producer? I can almost hear the thunderous applause now! **Think positively and let your success begin in your mind today and become a self-fulfilling prophecy!**

Chapter 19

INTERVIEW TECHNIQUE #2 ADVANCING

Once you have built trust with your prospects, it's time to start learning more about them. By doing an assessment of their situation, you will be in a position to make recommendations to help them accomplish their goals. You need to smoothly transition into a fact finding mode. **A good rule to follow is to explain the process and then get permission to proceed.** You have built up a trustful relationship, don't blow it here! You need to bridge to the next phase of the sales process: fact finding. Here are a few attempts you might try in order to get permission to proceed.

1. **"Is there anything we have not covered? Then, with your permission, let's get the process started..."** You can almost assume consent at that point and start asking some factual, non-threatening questions. It's a professional and soft-sell approach to transition from building trust to fact finding.

2. **"In order to determine whether, in fact, we can be of service to you, would it be okay to ask you some questions to get a clearer picture of your current situation?"** Here you are telling them exactly why you need to ask them some questions. You are not assuming they need anything right now—that's what your questions are going to help them determine.

3. **"I've noticed by the questions you've asked that there seems to be a real interest in proceeding. Is that correct?"** A "Yes" response and you're off and running. A negative response means you have more trust building to do.

4. **"Normally at this point I try to be quiet while you answer some important questions.** Are you comfortable with that?" That's really a soft sell approach, isn't it? Who would say, "No" to that question?

Earning the right to go to the next phase of the sales process is an important step. **Don't proceed without permission.** Earn it! Use a professional, well thought out approach to obtain your prospects' permission to proceed. It will bridge the gap from relationship building to fact finding very nicely.

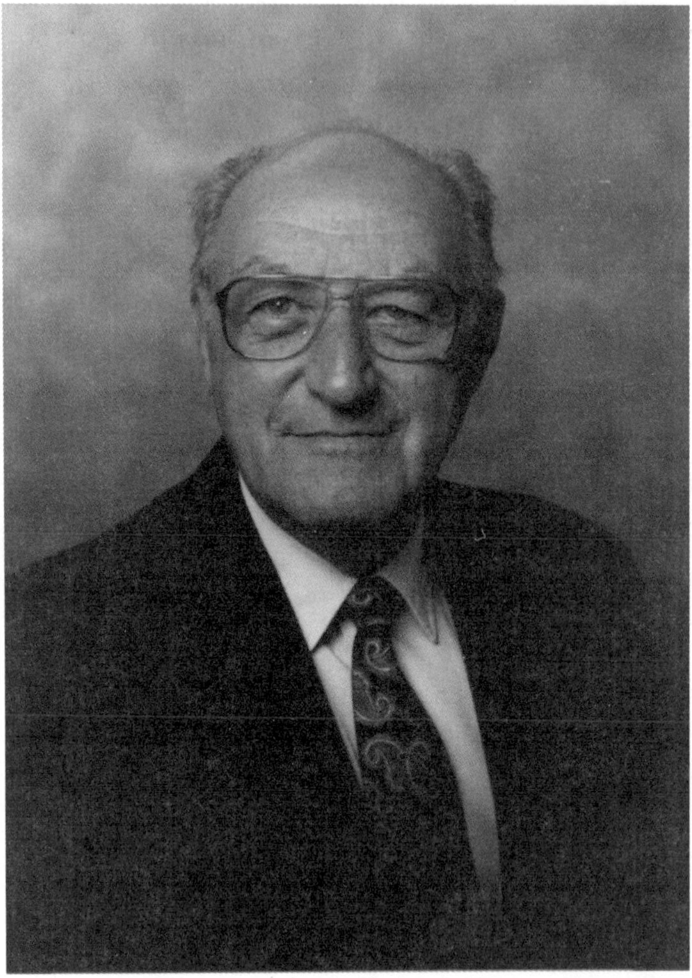

THIS CHAPTER IS DEDICATED TO
BOB STOVER

Bob "Smokey" Stover was my high school football coach. I know of no other person who loves the game of football like this man does. He elevated Lutheran West (Rocky River, OH) football to a pinnacle it has never since achieved. He had a passion for the game that few people could duplicate. He took the game pretty seriously. He was thorough in his preparation, tenacious in getting his team "up" for a game and a good "on the field" coach. The three seasons I played for Smokey, we went 24-5-1 with one loss in each of the last two seasons. We led the city of Cleveland in average points per game my junior year and most of the offensive school records still stand today after 30 years. While my name has been erased from the Lutheran West record book, the name of Bob Stover still stands prominently at the head of the list for most career victories by a coach.

Smokey was a leader. He demanded your respect. He was a disciplinarian. It was his way or the highway. Yet, he was a man of compassion who loved his players and would do anything to help them improve. He always tried to help his players get into college. After all these years he is still the first person I seek out when I know he is attending an athletic event.

Smokey, you demanded a lot of us and for that I thank you. You helped instill in me not only winning, but a winning attitude. Part of the intensity I possess, this thing called competitiveness, I attribute to your early tutelage. Your ability to focus rubbed off on me and I feel I am a better person because of your very positive influence. I was one of your captains my senior year and you helped me to develop leadership skills that still serve me well today. For that I thank you. Thank you, Smokey, for having confidence in me and for piloting the ship I was on from 1962-1965. It was a great journey! You have impacted my life in many ways and I thank you for your dedication, your positive influence and your leadership. I love you!

Dick

Chapter 20

"I WILL GREET THIS DAY WITH LOVE IN MY HEART"*

"Talk not of wasted affection! Affection never was wasted; If it enrich not the heart of another, its waters returning back to their springs, like the rain, shall fill them of refreshment: that which the fountain sends forth returns again to the fountain."
—Henry Wadsworth Longfellow

So much has been written about love that it would be difficult to come up with something very new or innovative. Jesus gave us a new paradigm when He said that it's not just loving your friends—that's easy—it's loving your enemies too. "I will greet this day with love in my heart." Just imagine the possibilities! Pessimism is converted to optimism. A kind word and a smile turns a cold glare into a friendly gaze. A few sincere compliments sprinkled throughout your day leave people feeling good about themselves. They in turn make others feel good too. **A rippling effect of love** spreads through workers, families and friends and transforms people into more caring and compassionate neighbors. A word of appreciation to a friend breeds stronger bonds and more loyal friendship. **You can't buy love and yet you can't give it away without getting it back in spades.**

Be bird-like. Greet this day with a song...a love song in your heart. Look forward to each day for the opportunities and the challenges. Not "another day, another dollar," but "another day to live life to its fullest." Another day in which to excel! "Good morning, Lord, thank you for this day." "This is the day which the Lord has made, let's rejoice and be glad today" (Psalm 118:24 GOD'S WORD). Don't waste time dwelling on past failures, pessimism, discontentment or discouragement. **Get high on life! Enthusiasm is contagious!** Greet this day with love in your heart. Watch people bask in your love and others blossom in your light.

If you could show love to everyone in your life every day, how different would your life be? How different would the world be? If love permeated everything you said and did, what kind of difference would it make with the people with whom you come in contact? Og Mandino said, "If I have not other qualities I can succeed with love alone. Without it I will fail though I posses all the knowledge and skills of the world." Agreed! A person could succeed in many selling careers by smiling a lot and seeing enough people. A smile indicates concern, warmth, caring and empathy. It goes a long way in developing a trusting and lasting relationship with another person. Are you as warm and loving as you could be? Would you like to be treated the way you treat others? Do you make a special effort to smile and turn on your genuine charm when meeting people? **Saturate others with your love.** Paul said it well when writing to the people of Corinth, **"Love is patient. Love is kind.** Love is not jealous. It doesn't sing it's own praises. It isn't arrogant. It isn't rude. It doesn't think about itself. It isn't irritable. It doesn't keep track of wrongs. It isn't happy when injustice is done, but it is happy with the truth. Love never stops being patient, never stops believing, never stops hoping, never gives up. So these three things remain: faith, hope, and love. But the best one of these is love. (I Corinthians 13:4-7, 13, GOD'S WORD)."

"I will greet this day with love in my heart!" Get a vision for the implications and potential that offers. Imagine how others will react to you and how you will be treated. What a difference it will make! What a joy to work with people in an atmosphere of mutual respect, empathy and compassion. If you greet this day with love in your heart, others will be compelled to react similarly to you. Stand back and watch love multiply itself again and again. Paul is right, "...but the best one of these is love."

* The title of the Scroll Marked II from Og Mandino's classic best seller *The Greatest Salesman in the World*, Lifetime Books Publisher

Chapter 21

INVITE DISSENT

"The trouble with most of us is that we would rather be ruined by praise than saved by criticism."
—Norman Vincent Peale

Confrontation doesn't happen to be my forte. I tend to avoid it like the plague. Maybe it has something to do with the fact that I had too many confrontations with upper classmen my first year at West Point (and of course you know who won those!). That's why when I heard a recent speaker say, "Invite dissent", it really got my attention. Frankly, it even made me cringe a little! On closer examination, however, I found there is great wisdom in those two words. "Invite" suggests that dissent is not only welcomed but even sought. "Dissent" is simply a different way of looking at or doing something. We should seek a difference of opinion, a new perspective, a unique approach. That's how we improve. That's how we initiate change. That's how we grow. **Invite dissent—welcome a different point of view.**

Periodically when our staff meets, I ask them to challenge everything we're doing. **Questioning why we're doing something a certain way is paramount to making changes and improvements.** Questioning yourself makes you either prove to yourself that something is worthwhile and should be continued, or else proves that it needs to be eliminated or changed. That's healthy! It's an effective way of not allowing yourself to get into ruts and staying there. It makes you get out of your comfort zone. It's not necessarily the West Point way, where tradition has a tendency of standing in the way of change. **When you are open for different opinions and welcome constructive criticism, you are demonstrating self-confidence and a belief in yourself.** You exhibit defensive behavior on the other hand when you take exception to dissent and fail to heed constructive criticism. While we're all probably guilty of this at times, it's best to keep it to a minimum.

Do you invite dissent? Do your interviews tend to be monologues? Or do you welcome participation and other viewpoints? Are you afraid of objections when you're trying to close a sale? Don't be!! **View them as a necessary step to find out exactly what your prospects are thinking and how they're feeling. Welcome them as a plea for more information.** You would never have gotten that far in the interview process if you didn't have an interested person. Now answering the objection is just the next step you need in order to close the transaction. Of course the earlier you invite dissent in the sales process, the better. You will be less likely then to get one during your "close". **Invite dissent; then listen.** Great advice. You'll be surprised what you learn.

Chapter 22

TEN WAYS TO SELF-DESTRUCT

"Good advice is one of those insults that ought to be forgiven."
—Author Unknown

1. Always work from your agenda rather than your client's. You know what's important. They don't.
2. Talk more than listen—after all you're the knowledgeable one.
3. Never ask a question you don't know the answer to—that way you can manipulate your client.
4. Don't spend too much time preparing for the interview because you're good at "winging it".
5. Return every phone call on Friday. That's a good catch up day anyway.
6. Always use abbreviations (it's quicker) and talk your jargon; that will help educate them.
7. A yellow pad approach is probably best since people hate high tech stuff anyway.
8. Stay as long as you want because people want relationships.
9. Always tell them your latest joke—even if it's a little off-color, that will lighten them up a little.
10. Don't make people feel too important or they'll start expecting something extra.

Any one of these could lead to disaster. **Be careful. Don't self-destruct. Be intentional about everything you do.**

Chapter 23

WHAT'S YOUR FAILURE RATE?

"If I could have one hope for our young people as they go out into the world, it would be this: I hope they fail. I hope they fail at something that is important to them, for failure, like nothing else, is able to stimulate the right kind of person to that extra action that always makes all the difference."
—Lyman Fertig

Have you failed lately? I hope so! If not, then maybe you should heed the advice of Thomas J. Watson, the founder of IBM, who once made this statement, "Do you want to be successful? Then double your failure rate."

What great advice—double your failure rate! **People generally never fail in sales because of the people they don't sell. They fail because of the people they don't see.** So if you want to succeed, double your failure rate. The logic is unmistakable. If a person closes one out of every three prospects and has six closing interviews a week, he or she will close two cases. Duh! If that person doubles the number of people he or she sees, then they'll close four cases. I did that without a calculator!

Look at any sports record setter and it will prove Mr. Watson's statement. The sport of hockey and the "Great One," Wayne Gretzky, are almost synonymous. Gretzky holds the record for most goals scored in the history of the NHL as well as most total points. Not surprisingly he holds some other records of more dubious distinction—most shots taken and missed for one. Gretzky simply failed his way to success. Pete Rose has more singles and total hits than anyone in baseball history (maybe bets too!). He also holds the record for most outs. Charlie Hustle failed his way to success. Rose doesn't have the highest batting average of all time, but he persisted and persisted until he accomplished feats that may never be broken.

The fact is that to succeed in anything involves risk. A person must be willing to risk failure in order to have the opportunity to succeed. How often in sports competition do you see teams lose games they should not have lost because they got too complacent or conservative? The big lead that they built up probably came by aggressive and creative plays. Then once they built that big lead they, "took the air out of the ball", they "sat on the lead", or just decided to "play it close to the vest". Basically, they stopped risking. Instead of playing the game to win, they played the game not to lose. That reminds me of the Confucius saying, "He who wants to make a splash in the puddle of life must be willing to jump."

Success in sales is very measurable. It's easy to look at your income or the number of sales you had or a dollar volume and determine just how "successful" you were in a given year. You're not graded on attempts to sell, the number of people you saw or the number of times you attempted to close in a particular interview. That's too bad! You know what? You'd probably find the results about the same.

Most successful salespeople don't have any magical "closes" that they alone possess that will lead to sales in every interview. In most cases they don't have extra special skills and talents compared to other salespeople. **They simply have**

learned to see enough people each week so they can fail their way to success. The "great ones" in sales insure their success by keeping their calendars filled with people to see. They keep in mind the philosophy that **the harder they work, the luckier they get.** Great philosophy! Make your own breaks! Fail your way to success by doubling your failure rate. You're bound to find what others have found—it's worth the effort.

Have you failed lately? I hope so!

Chapter 24

TAKE THIS JOB AND......LOVE IT!

"To love what you do and feel that it matters—how could anything be more fun?"
—Katherine Graham

Have you had a tough day recently? Probably a silly question in a selling career! We all have them. As sure as day follows night we're bound to have a real bummer once in a while. What you do about it says more about your character and your chances for success in sales than the fact that you had one. Selling is a very unique career whether you're selling life insurance, industrial supplies or screen doors. You will either learn to bounce back after a setback or two (or three...) or you will not survive and succeed in this career. Rejection and "No's" are par for the course. They are part of a normal day. Having said that, let's not feel too sorry for ourselves. This can be a great career for the right person. We don't have to rely on anyone else for our success. We don't have to play corporate politics. No one is telling you that you can only earn $___ (you fill in the blank), if you're in commission sales. You have almost complete freedom and independence to work when you want and how you want. Usually **the more people you help the more successful you will be.** How incredible! **You work in a job where you get paid to help people.** That's fantastic! Think of that the next time you've had ten people in a row say "No!" to you on the phone. Remember that when you get stood up for an appointment. Setbacks? Sure, but every job is going to have some unpleasant tasks or features you don't like. Disappointments? Absolutely! But they'll pale in comparison to the tangible and intangible rewards that come with connecting with people and helping them through the sale of your products or services. Why not just take this job and love it!

Getting a little down about your job? How about trading places with someone who has an "ordinary 9 to 5" job? What do they do when they want to take some family time during the day? What can they do to increase their income by 10-15% next year? Can they control some of the variables involved in work like you can? Things like schedules, where to work, how to do the job, when to do the job and when to take a break? Still feeling a little down because you've come to one of life's speed bumps? You've probably heard the expression, "You can complain about the shoes you wear until you see the person who has no feet." There is more than just a grain of truth in it. We are so blessed! Your attitude is everything! Flat on your back? Pick yourself up, dust yourself off and get right back in the race. **Remember all the worthwhile things in life come through hard work and perseverance.** Hang in there! **Attitude is everything!** The pessimist says, "Good God, morning?" The optimist says, "Good morning, God!" What a difference your attitude makes. Have you had a tough day? So what? I bet you won't go hungry tonight. Tomorrow is coming and a new day is dawning. Another day in which to excel! Why not just take this job and love it! One of life's miracles is that God enables ordinary people (like you and me) to do extraordinary things. Go for it!

If you can't seem to shake that negative attitude, perhaps you're in the wrong occupation after all. Maybe it would be best to get out of selling and into an "ordinary" career. Maybe you lack the intestinal fortitude and perseverance to be successful in selling. Maybe you don't have the self-discipline to come back and make more phone calls after you've had your share of rejection. No sense kidding yourself any longer. **Life's too short to work at a job you don't really love.** Good luck in your evaluation. Most of you will probably come to the conclusion that despite some of the negatives of your career, the freedom and independence are worth all of the little frustrations that come with a sales career. It's free enterprise at its best. **If you've come to the conclusion that it isn't so bad after all, then why not just take this job and love it!**

This chapter is dedicated to the memory of my brother, Robert W. Luecke, killed in action in Vietnam on March 2, 1968. This was written 25 years later on March 2, 1993.

Chapter 25

REFLECTIONS

"What peaceful hours I once enjoy'd!
How sweet their memory still!
But they have left an aching void
The world can never fill."
—William Cowper

Do you know how some dates and times are kind of etched in your mind forever and ever? Like exactly where were you when you learned JFK had been shot?...or when Neil Armstrong took "One small step for man, one giant leap for mankind"? March 2, 1968 is one of those dates for me. Somehow twenty-five years have elapsed and yet it's a date I cannot erase from my mind. The thing is, it started out to be a great day for me. A brisk but bright day dawned for me with great expectations at West Point. Weekend Leave at 12 Noon! After room inspections, Saturday morning classes, and a short parade in the "Area", I was finally free for a 30 hour weekend leave. My favorite uncle picked me up by the chapel as he usually did and we had no problems making New York City and a visit to Madison Square Garden to watch the Rangers in a 2:00 P.M. matinee hockey game. Then we went back to his home in New Jersey (my home away from home) for a home cooked meal and some R & R. Meanwhile, halfway around the world in Vietnam, my role model, mentor, leader, friend, and brother was being cut down by enemy fire. It was the Tet Offensive of 1968. On March 2, 1968 I lost my hero. The one person who most influenced my life was gone. The person I looked up to and loved so much was dead. My brother, Bob, gone forever? It couldn't be! No more fun times together? No more double dates? No more telegrams from him before football games ("It will be a genuine thrill for me to see you in person in your first Army football game. Stop. Good luck against V.M.I. Stop. Your biggest fan. Stop. Bob")? It can't be! We had too much to share yet!

 I didn't find out about it for a couple of days. Even then when my Dad called he said that the Army reported Bob only as "missing in action". Everyone at West Point knew what that meant—he was gone. That's the Army's way of preparing you for the inevitable bad news which follows. Despite the news I somehow tried to cling to a shred of hope that maybe, just maybe, this would be an exception. Within two days my Dad called again and confirmed our worst fears—Bob was dead.

 The days that followed remain a blur. Home for a weekend leave to try to comfort and console my broken hearted parents and brother Randy. Then the wait. It took over three weeks for Bob's body to be shipped back home. It was an agonizing and awful wait. Nothing seemed to matter much. Classes at West Point went on. Conditioning drills for football came and went. Friends and other cadets and officers offered condolences. Frequent phone calls to grieving and concerned parents. Just one day at a time. How could life go on when we were hurting so much? Then, finally, Bob was home. We saw him one last time. A memorial service at Bethany, our church, was tough on everyone. But the toughest part of all was Bob's funeral and burial at West Point and the playing of Taps. The finality of it all was almost too much to bear.

I knew at the time that no one was hurting as much as I was. After all, we were very close. Didn't I follow in Bob's footsteps to West Point? Didn't Bob help me get through that Plebe Year at West Point? And wasn't it Bob who came hurriedly to seek me out immediately after the Graduation Parade to congratulate me on finishing that first year? My goodness how I loved him! Didn't I select Ft. Bragg for training the summer of 1967 so that I could be with Bob during that month? No one could miss him more. In time, I found out first hand that it wasn't that way at all. When I became a parent I truly found out that a brother's love for a brother could not compare to a parent's love for a son. It was then that I began to realize just how much my parents must have suffered at that time. And even though perhaps I was closer to Bob (at least age wise) than Randy, he still loved Bob as much as I did.

It's been 25 years, Bob, that you've been gone. While my treks to your grave sight at West Point are less frequent now than the weekly visits that first year, I still miss you very much. Sometimes I feel ashamed and guilty for what I was doing on that March 2nd day when you were giving the supreme sacrifice for your country. But I know you wouldn't have wanted it any other way. Sometimes I still shed tears of grief, of joy, of love, of memories, of bitterness, of agony, of pain. Trying to sing "What a Friend We Have in Jesus" will certainly do it every time. And sometimes I still just wonder why it was you instead of me.

I so much wish the people reading this could have known you like I knew you. I wish our boys could have known their Uncle Bob. I wish you could have experienced the love of a woman like I have with Linda. I wish you could have observed our parents maturing gracefully.

It's been 25 years, Bob, and I still miss you and still remember all that you did for me. Most of all though, I remember how proud you were of me and how much you loved me. I only wish you knew how very proud we all are of you and how much we still love you.

                                        Your Brother,

                                        Dick

Chapter 26

"I WILL PERSIST UNTIL I SUCCEED"*

"Ride on! Rough-shod if need, smooth-shod if that will do, but ride on! Ride on over all obstacles, and win the race!"

—Charles Dickens

Chances are some other people at work have more talent than you do. There is nothing you can do about that. Talent is simply God-given ability. You just have to make sure that you're using what God has given to you.

Chances are there are probably people who have more experience than you do. That's just a matter of longevity. Some people can get ten years of experience in three years through hard work while others take fifteen years to acquire that same ten years of experience.

Chances are some people just happen to have better skill than you. Maybe their training was better. Maybe they've been exposed to great mentors. Maybe they had better technology with which to work.

Chances are pretty good that there are people who have greater knowledge than you do. They've spent more time in school, had better teachers, learned things quicker, and possess better retention skills.

Chances are that other people have better "connections" than you do. They have a natural market. They do a good job of networking. They are involved in a lot of outside activities and just happen to know a lot of people.

75

Do talent, experience, skill, knowledge, and connections help a person to be successful? Even a fool will know the answer to that question. Absolutely! But a person could have all of those things and yet not be successful on a long term basis without one more key ingredient. Persistence! **Without persistence most people will fail.** Persistence is one of the most underrated qualities which all successful people possess.

Persistence can show up in a thousand different ways. Doing a few more of the unpleasant tasks before calling it a day. Never settling for less than your intended goal—working until you've reached it. Going the extra mile for a customer when others would not have. Not giving up on that big account despite all the "hoops" they're asking you to jump through. Caring enough to contact customers even when you don't anticipate any current sales situations developing. **Never stopping at the bare minimum expectations but going till you've surpassed your goal.** The list could go on and on.

You can give yourself that key ingredient. It's not like some of the other ingredients mentioned above. You can do it by removing from your vocabulary words like: cannot, unable, impossible, improbable, and phrases like: "I tried that once", "I quit", and "that will never work". You can give yourself that key ingredient by working at being more consistent and developing winning habits. **You can give yourself that key ingredient by keeping focused on your goal, being committed to it and ignoring all the little obstacles that are bound to come your way.**

Calvin Coolidge summarized it very well when he said, "Nothing in the world can take the place of persistence. Talent will not; nothing is more common than unsuccessful men with talent. Genius will not; unrewarded genius is almost a proverb. Education will not; the world is full of educated derelicts. Persistence and determination alone are omnipotent. The slogan 'press on' has solved and always will solve the problems of the human race."

Persistence. Give yourself that key ingredient and watch how success will hound you. **Go the extra mile**—it will be a lonely stretch. **Develop that mental toughness** that no one can really give you or teach you. Persistence must be earned one effort at a time. **One deliberate, intentional act**—there's that word again—upon another will set you apart from all others and set you on a course that will end up on the victory stand. Winston Churchill's famous graduation speech bears repeating. "Never. Never. Never. Never. Never give up."

* The title of the Scroll Marked III from Og Mandino's classic best seller, *The Greatest Salesman in the World,* Lifetime Books Publisher

Chapter 27

"NO EXCUSE, SIR!"

"There are a thousand reasons for failure, but not a single excuse."

—Mike Read

When a ship misses the harbor, it is never the harbor's fault! Do you sometimes blame "the harbor" for some of your failures? It's easy and tempting to do in sales, isn't it?

"It's the economy that's bad."

"Interest rates are causing people to stay on the sidelines."

"My company isn't delivering the product quickly enough."

"We don't have the cheapest product, you know."

"My products aren't as good as XYZ Company."

"People just aren't in a buying mood."

"Everyone is putting me off till after the holidays."

"The government's latest report...." etc., etc.

Oh, we can sure think of a million excuses alright. Rationalizations for why we don't succeed. Yet, every year salespeople in our same industry are making record sales. Hmmmmm, I wonder if it could be my fault?

My first year at West Point was a memorable one. Frankly, that's unfortunate, because I'd rather forget it. One thing which remains vividly clear to me was my first day at school.

That wasn't late August or the beginning of September like most schools, but the 1st of July. You see, we had a little two month indoctrination period called "New Cadet Barracks." That was the official name. The cadets affectionately called it "Beast Barracks". It was well earned. So July 1st as I embarked on my collegiate career, I found out that I had four answers to questions by upperclassmen (yes, just men then—I'm that old!). The answers were:

"Yes, sir!"

"No, sir!"

"No excuse, sir!" and

"Sir, I do not understand!"

That was easy enough to learn. Easy, because if you didn't respond with one of those four answers, you'd think you just started World War III. You'd have upperclassmen all over you barking out insults and making you feel lower than a snake. Great environment! It was easy to learn the four answers but sometimes very hard to follow. There were always "reasons" why my shoes weren't properly shined. Or "reasons" why I was tardy. Or "reasons" why my belt buckle had a smudge on it. Or "reasons" why I missed my first ever Reveille Formation (boy, did that cost me dearly!). And I sure wanted to be able to explain to my squad leader why I didn't have time to learn all the movies for the week and who starred in them, and what time they were playing and where. I knew better! I'd just say, "No excuse, sir!" and face the consequences. That was what the life of a Plebe was like. But it wasn't all bad. **I learned to take responsibility for my failures.** I learned that my

decisions and choices always had consequences. It was hammered home in many ways thousands of times that first year in college. And yes, thank God, it did eventually come to an end! I still find myself off course and missing the harbor every now and then (what do you want, I was in the Army not the Navy!). But I'm not likely to blame the harbor. Instead I'll just remember, "No excuse, sir!" and take my consequences. I recognize that most failures or setbacks are of my own doing. Harbors don't move! I take credit for my victories and I can take credit for the losses too. I'm a big boy. I don't need excuses.

So the next time you're about to blame the harbor, don't. Instead, **accept personal responsibility and take the consequences.** While there are probably plenty of "reasons" for something bad happening, don't be tempted to hide behind them. Remember, "No excuse, sir!", and you'll probably feel a whole lot better than blaming someone else. "Yes, sir!"

Chapter 28

INTERVIEW TECHNIQUE #3 FACT FINDING

Having built trust and earned the right to ask questions, it's time to gather some information. You probably have a fact finding form that will help you gather the information relative to their situation and specific for your particular type of sales. **It should consist of both factual information as well as feeling type questions.** What you want to do during this phase of the interview process is determine **where your prospects are**—their current situation—and **where they would like to be**—their ideal situation. The bigger the "gap" between the current and the ideal situations, the more motivated your prospects should be to solve their problem—the "gap". **Their ideal situation is simply their goals and objectives; their dreams.** In a family financial situation it could be funding their children's college education or adequate retirement income. In a computer sales interview with a law firm, it might be the latest technology which will allow attorneys, secretaries and legal assistants to all be linked together with complete access to legal decisions and tax law rulings.

Good fact finding is probably the most underrated phase of the sales process. While most salespeople are good at building rapport and trust with prospects, my experience shows that **most sales are lost because of inadequate fact finding.** Asking good questions and being a good listener are imperative during this phase. People will do things for their reasons, not ours, therefore it is our responsibility to find out exactly what they want and why. Good questions are key to finding out what they will buy. People will generally **tell you exactly what they want if you ask them professionally.** This information will then help you build and construct a case for what you're going to recommend. The key is to ask the right question and then be silent. **Listen. Listen. Listen.** It's one of the hardest things for most salespeople to master. It is imperative during this phase of the interview to be a "gifted" listener. Listen empathetically to try to capture the feelings of your prospects as well as insights into their motivations.

After listening and gathering the pertinent information, **it is important to give your prospects feedback on what you heard.** A quick summary of their situation as well as a prioritized list of their goals and objectives will demonstrate to them how good a listener you have been. This will go a long way toward building even greater trust and the start of a beneficial long term relationship. Since you now know what your prospects want, you are in a good position to offer products or services to solve their problem. And that's the next step.

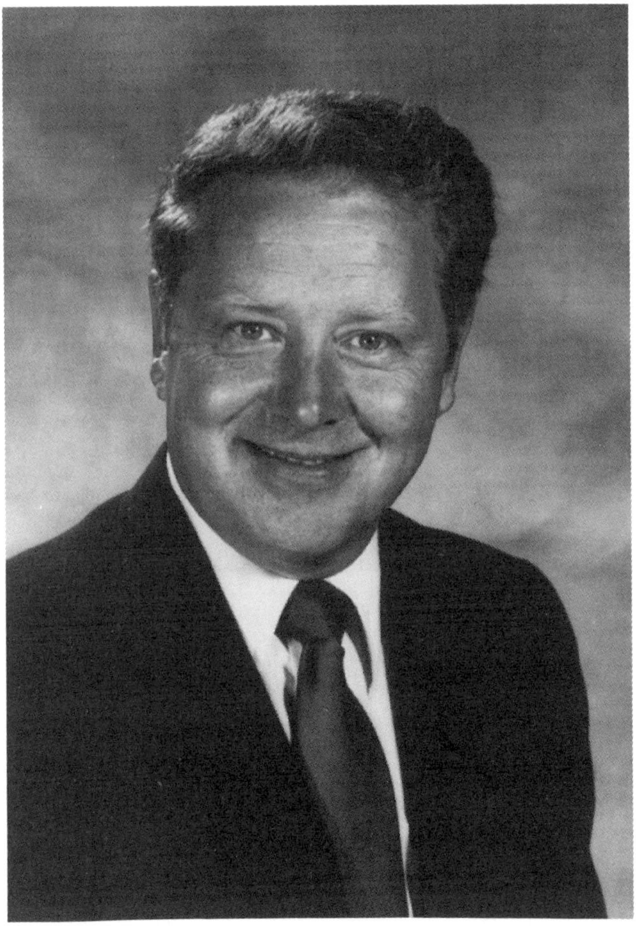

THIS CHAPTER IS DEDICATED TO
DICK LINN

When I was an impressionable young man (at least a couple of years ago now!) a person entered my life who was a great role model for me. He was my high school biology teacher, my freshman football and basketball coach and my ride to and from school every day. While I certainly didn't dazzle him in the classroom (would you believe a C?), I think I was able to contribute to some of his athletic coaching successes. What a privilege it was for this freshman to ride together with Dick Linn and three seniors. The three seniors were all in leadership positions in the high school (Student Council President, Vice President and Senior Class President) and included my brother, Bob. Those were certainly memorable trips! It all ended rather abruptly when Dick had the audacity to get married and move out of Parma, OH. Dick Linn was someone you could look up to, someone you could respect and someone you could really like all at the same time. You know what? I still do! After more than 30 years, like the Eveready rabbit, he keeps going and going and...

To me, Dick Linn represents everything good about a Lutheran high school education. He is tough and demanding in the classroom. He has high standards and expects a lot from his students. He is a good role model for young people to follow. His career has never been tainted by unbecoming behavior, unsavory company or a compromising of his Christian principles. When he was asked to serve as Principal, he sacrificed personal goals for the good of the school and he accepted. When alumni return to their alma mater, Dick Linn is probably the first person they ask about or seek out. After all these years Dick remains a pillar at Lutheran West in Rocky River, Ohio.

Dick, for your commitment to the ministry of educating young people, I salute you, commend you, and thank you. For remaining faithful to your calling and faithful to your Lord I say, "Well done!" For all you have done for me over the years I also say, "Thank you!" You influenced me in a very positive manner for four full years in high school. You were a hero to me then and still are today. In Lutheran High circles you have become a legend. Our families have grown together over the years and you are certainly a respected and admired friend. The only difference between high school and today is that I now set picks for your son rather than you (that's basketball talk!). I want you to know how blessed I am because of your positive influence. Thanks for being such a good role model for me first, and now for our sons. It's a privilege to call you my friend. I love you!

Dick

Chapter 29

.. AND THEN SOME!

"What you get, you earn with diligence and intelligence. It's amazing how lucky you get after working on something long after others have given up. Success — it's easier than you think!"

—Bryant Gumbel

Some would argue that Raymond Berry had the best work ethic of anyone who ever played the game of professional football. That of course is a bold statement and is a very arguable opinion. Berry was a wide receiver who played for the old Baltimore Colts (not the Ravens!) during the Johnny Unitas era. He wasn't fast. He wasn't even quick. The thick glasses he wore were an enigma in the ranks of professional football. He wasn't blessed with great talent. The thing he did better than anyone else playing the game was that he worked his butt off.... and then some. He was a perfectionist. After every practice he made Johnny U. throw extra passes to him. When Unitas' arm grew weary he'd cajole a backup quarterback or coach to throw a few more... and then some. He was untiring in his quest for perfection. He raised the sideline pass catch to an artform. The great receivers of today probably can thank him for the honing of their skills because of his great example of perfection. He was a tireless worker who just may have gotten more out of his God-given talent than anyone who ever played the game. He did that by paying his dues .... and then some.

People throughout recorded history have shown they could overcome immense odds and unbelievable obstacles and succeed magnificently by working hard .... and then some. **Those three little words .... and then some .... capture the essence of true resolve, undeniable determination, and a passionate work ethic.** It can't be measured. It's even difficult to evaluate. It can't be passed down from one generation to the next. It's not even taught in our schools. We can only hope to learn from those who demonstrate this rare gift. Those three words embody the indomitable spirit and the heart of champions.

Let me introduce you to Ben Feldman. New York Life Insurance Company turned down the application for employment of this squatty man who spoke with a slight lisp. Ben didn't accept no for an answer, however, and the rest is history. He went on to write and re-write the record book for sales year after year for the life insurance industry. At his peak he wrote more insurance in a year than over half of the insurance companies in the United States. How did he do it? With fierce determination and a work ethic that wouldn't allow for anything but his very best .... and then some.

Want a sure-fire formula for success? **Just add those three words to any goal you may have.** Learn as much as you can ....and then some. See as many people as you can .... and then some. Work as hard as you can .... and then some. Remember when going the extra mile there's never much traffic. Many people stop when success is within easy grasp.

Go the extra mile .... and then some. Give it your best shot .... and then some. If you do, you're sure to be among the top salespeople or near the top in any field of endeavor.

Chapter 30

SMOOTH SAILING

"When one door closes, another opens. But we often look so long and so regretfully upon the closed door that we do not see the one which has opened for us."
— Alexander Graham Bell

There's an African proverb that goes like this, "Smooth seas do not make skillful sailors." I like that. If you read between the lines it's saying that unless you have had a little adversity in your life and experienced some rough spots, you probably aren't as wise or as skillful as someone who has. There's sure a lot of evidence to support that. While we don't go looking for "rough seas" or adversity, **when we have faced them we usually emerge stronger and wiser from the experience.** There are lots of applications to anyone in a sales position. Have you ever lost a big case to the competition? Have you ever lost a customer because of poor service? Have you ever lost a case because you didn't follow up on some of the details as you should have? Have you ever missed a sale because your timing was off (you forgot when you were supposed to contact the customer)? Have you ever missed a paycheck because of some failure on your part? If you haven't experienced any of these "rough seas", then you probably haven't been in sales very long. Actually, we face a fair amount of adversity in this business as a matter of course. We constantly face rejection, getting stood up, appointment postponements, cancellations and even losing a case because of "problems" which arise after the sale has already been made. The question certainly isn't "will you experience these things?" We all will. **The question is "how will we respond to them when they do occur?" You have a choice.** You can get discouraged, distracted and let them immobilize you. Or, you can accept them as part of the ups and downs of this business and react positively. It's a certainty that no one likes the adversities or "rough seas" of our lives. **We must, however, for our long term success, respond positively and grow from the experience.**

There are some things which we should never accept. We should never accept inefficiency or sloppiness. We should never accept lack of effort or lack of follow-through on our part, or lack of responsiveness to our customers. Those must always be top priority. What we must learn to accept is the fact that there are some variables in this business that we have no control over whatsoever. **Rather than focusing on these negatives, focus on the things you can control.** It will make a huge difference. Adversities? Naturally! Rough seas? Of course! But you'll be a better sailor than the sailor who had smooth seas. And that piece of advice comes from an Army man!

Chapter 31

A NEW KIND OF PATRIOT

"Eternal vigilance is the price of liberty."
— Thomas Jefferson

July 4th—Independence Day! A day to celebrate our nation's birthday. A day to commemorate our great American heritage. A day to reflect on the commitments and sacrifices of our founding fathers. A day to ponder again all the personal freedoms we enjoy as Americans. A day to contemplate our country as the great melting pot of the world. A day to meditate on what a democracy is and what wonderful opportunities we have in a free enterprise system. A day to appreciate the ability we have to determine our own success or failure and the capability to chart our own destiny. No where else on the face of the earth exists such opportunities and freedoms.

Will it be back to business as usual on July 5th? Look around you and what do you see? Education systems crumbling. Unparalleled suicide rates among young people. The destruction of the traditional American family unit. Rampant violent crime. Pornography. Over thirty million abortions. Budget deficits and soaring national debt. A court system that often caters to criminals. Unethical and unconscionable politicians. Leaders lacking in both integrity and vision. Biased behavior and discrimination among races. And the beat goes on and on.

Change is needed not only in the nation's capital but throughout the land. We can no longer accept this pathway to degradation, corruption and scandal. We can no longer accept total disregard for fiscal restraint and responsibility. We must find private cures for our youth and our educational system. We must insist on accountability. We must revamp our courts so that we protect and reward victims rather than the criminals. We must change the course of human history. We must return to a nation that accepts the premise "In God We Trust." At this point we need divine intervention. We need a national revival. **We need a new kind of patriot.**

A new kind of patriot will impact our country as never before. A new kind of patriot will do the following:

1. **Be responsible.** It all begins with you and me. We must 'walk our talk'. **We must take personal responsibility for our lives.** We must live within our means. We must support our local charities. We must be model citizens. We must not use the system, but rather be productive and support the system.
2. **Be informed.** Keep your eyes and ears open. **Stay tuned to the heartbeat of America.** Know how your Senators and Representative vote on the issues. Read responsible commentataries and editorials of good writers. Attend lectures of respected experts. Subscribe to newsletters of respected authors. Know where you stand on the issues. Let C-SPAN be your channel of choice.
3. **Be heard.** Your voice is important. Write to government officials. **Stand up and be counted.** Let leaders know who you are and let them hear from you often. Be in touch with your Senators and Representative. Participate when possible in debates, meetings and discussions. Seek public participation.

4. **Be in prayer.** Nothing will make change in this country occur faster than the will of God. Seek His will for our lives. **Pray diligently for our country.** Ask God to forgive our country for our sins. Pray that God-fearing leaders with vision will be raised up to lead us from this rubble.

A new day is dawning in America. It's no longer okay for us to sit by and watch all the radical groups which are out of the mainstream of American values and principles clamor for media attention. Passive behavior has helped get us where we are today. **Now we must unite and be heard.** We must rise up and let our elected officials know that morality and integrity and personal responsibility are all the order of the day. No more lambs. **The new patriots must be lions and eagles.** We must be bold and unrelenting and change the course of our country now. May God bless the new patriots and reward us with a country of integrity, values, and honor.

Chapter 32

"....AND THE TIMES THEY ARE A CHANGIN"

"World knowledge doubles every four years. Everyone becomes automatically obsolete within that short period of time, unless a serious and determined effort is made, consistently and constructively, to remain current and knowledgeable. Maintaining one's competence and the infusion of new knowledge is essential in an era of fast change and unpredictability. Self-education should be priority one on anyone's list."

—Michael Kami

The old Bob Dylan song from the 1960's has never been more true. The times are indeed, changing. **Constant change.** That's an oxymoron none of us should forget. That sure became evident to me recently when I learned I had cancer. My 'wake up call' made me realize more than ever not only how fragile life is, but how quickly things can change. Things are changing in all areas of our lives. The pace has quickened with no end in sight. To put things into perspective about how rapidly things are changing let me share with you a quote from one of my favorite authors (despite the fact that he's from the Naval Academy), Denis Waitley, who said, "Today, when I throw away a musical birthday card, I am tossing out more computer power than existed in the entire world before 1948." Unbelievable! Things are changing so fast it's sometimes hard to keep up, isn't it? Don't you just want to say, "Whoa! Let's not change anything for the next six months so that I can catch up." Unfortunately we don't have that luxury. Unfortunately we can't just say, "Stop the world I want to get off."

We really need to embrace change like never before. That's a lot easier said than done. It's hard to embrace anything when you're working hard at making a living in a career. But do it, we must. We need to stay in a positive mode in relationship to things changing 'round about us.' Let's accept the premise that while not all change is necessarily good, most is. **Most change improves something.** Technological changes allow us to be more efficient, retrieve information more quickly, speed up transactions, spend more time with our customers, respond quicker to customers, target specific audiences, be more creative, improve presentations, be more consistent and persistent and even learn more effectively. That's quite a list of improvements, isn't it? But just consider where we were just a few short years ago. Now we even get impatient when we don't have the fastest computer at our disposal and the screens don't move quickly enough. Just realize how much marketing has changed over the last five years. You used to be able to reach people for appointments by telephone at home. No more. You better not plan on making too many "cold calls" anymore. Unsolicited phone calls may become illegal before long. In the meantime, however, it's pretty tough now to reach anyone due to answering machines which people use to screen phone calls. Add to that caller ID programs and it's going to become virtually impossible. If you've relied on reaching people at home via the phone, **you need to change the way you're doing business through seminars, networking, and referrals.**

So the challenge isn't, "Should we change?" The challenge is, "How exactly can we take advantage of all the new improvements and innovative ideas?" You have to figure out the answer to that question. There is no easy solution. Here are at least a few suggestions:

1. **Stay in a pro-active mode in relationship to change** as much as possible. Don't resist it—embrace it!

2. **Identify your major sources of initiating change.** My list would be—my Home Office, Million Dollar Round Table, General Agents and Managers Association, Tom Peters and John Nesbitt books, and two or three periodicals. What is yours? Keep your eyes and ears open for innovative thinking and change initiatives.

3. **Designate a time during the week or month when you will devote some time to change.** Use this time to think creatively, learn and adopt change.

4. **Seek mentors to challenge you, build you, lead you and inspire you.** Everyone knows people who are at a higher level in their careers than we are in ours. Seek them out and ask them for help. Chances are they're probably on the cutting edge of change.

Bob Dylan was right, "The times they are a-changin" indeed! **Rapid, constant and meteoric change are with us to stay. It's an exciting time to be living!** Change simply permeates every aspect of our lives today. **Embrace it or regret it—the choice is yours!**

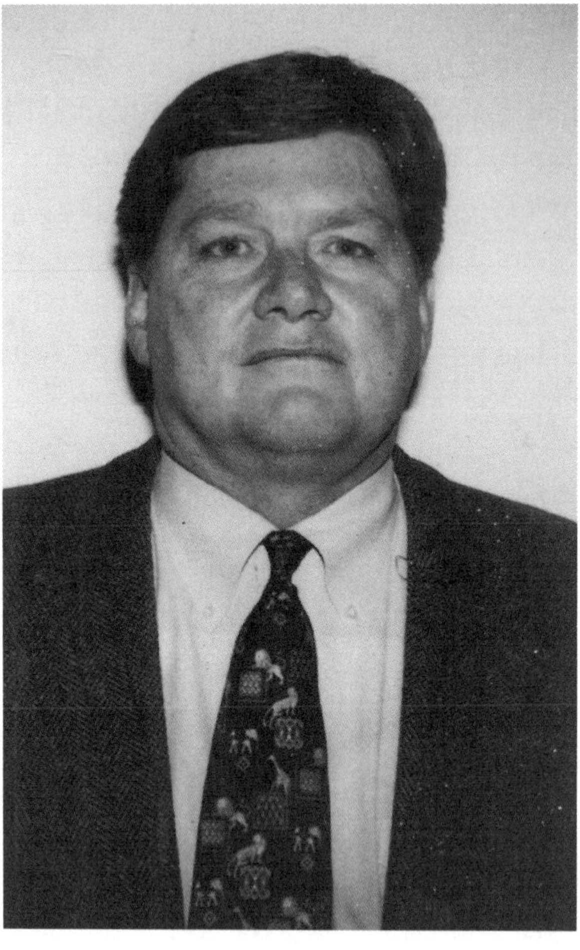

THIS CHAPTER IS DEDICATED TO
NED DOYLE

Ned "Tucker" Doyle was my roommate for three years at West Point. To say we were close friends would be like saying the Pope is a little Catholic. We were inseparable. "Luck and Tuck" they used to call us. After graduation we went through Jump Shool together as partners and were even Ranger Buddies in the Army's Ranger School. Then it was off to Germany with our brides where we served in the same unit and lived not more than three miles from each other.

No one influenced my life more at West Point than Ned. We had no secrets; our lives were open books to each other. Anything could be said without concern that the other person would be judgmental. When my brother Bob was killed in Vietnam, no one was more supportive, more concerned or more compassionate than Ned was. We grieved together. That's how life was back then. We shared each other's joys and triumphs and commiserated in each other's setbacks and tragedies. Academically we both struggled. I taught him all I knew which made us both deficient academically-the blind leading the blind! No matter how hard the academics got or how tough the spartan, disciplined life of those Cadet days, Ned's steady banter, humorous expressions and constant worry saw us through. His expressions were priceless! There never seemed to be a dull moment, that's for certain! His academic achievements not withstanding, Ned was a standout on the Army Hockey team as a two year letterman. I was there watching him the day he banged into the boards causing a separated shoulder. His passion for the ice was only surpassed by his great passion for Patty who has been his roommate for the past 27 years.

Tuck, your strong faith in God (Mass every morning at 6:20 A.M.), Bostonian accent, quick smile and sense of humor became your trademarks and made you a popular classmate. I knew you more intimately. I got to see the real Ned Doyle. What I saw was a person who really cared about other people. What I saw was a person with high values, strong ethical convictions and a burning desire to succeed. You made me feel like a better person just being around you.

Ned, thanks for the support you've always given me. Thanks for all the good times we've shared over the years. Thanks for influencing me in so many positive ways. Thanks for making our time at West Point meaningful, eventful and bearable. Without your sense of humor and your ability to put things in proper perspective, it would have been a whole lot tougher. I'll always love you and I'll always cherish our friendship.

Dick

Chapter 33

INTEGRITY: YOUR CODE OF ETHICS

"I would like to impress upon young people the importance of honesty and integrity. If they have both, they'll never want for anything in life. The other less important things—the material things—will follow."
—Gib Shanley, Sportscaster

Where I went to school the Honor Code summed it up very well: "A cadet does not lie, cheat nor steal, nor tolerate one who does." It was a great environment in which to live. We didn't have locks on our doors. You could take a person at his word. You didn't worry about someone peeking over your shoulder during an exam. It was one of the most competitive environments you could ever imagine, and yet one of the most honest environments too. It was great! The Honor Code was one of the most hallowed and revered traditions at a school rather steeped in tradition. It taught moral character, ethical behavior, honesty under pressure and consequences of your choices. It also taught leadership by example. The political leaders of our country could learn a great deal about moral character and integrity by observing the cadets.

Integrity in all your business transactions and contact with your customers is an absolute imperative. Your sales career begins and ends with trust. It is the cornerstone of every relationship you establish. It is an essential ingredient of your success. If trust is lacking, everything else you do will be undermined and sabotaged. It even goes beyond honesty. Honesty is merely the starting point. **Integrity involves doing what is right for your customers 100% of the time.** It means a commitment on your part to top flight service. It means a commitment to continued growth and development in your professional career. **Integrity means putting your customers' needs before your own needs.** It means going the extra mile for your customers. It's doing as much as you can to help and serve every customer assigned to you. Integrity is constantly making the tough choices. It's choosing right over expedience. It's choosing to serve rather than being served.

A person's character and true integrity are revealed in the confines of their own minds. **Character is what you do when no one else is looking. Integrity is being true to yourself.** It's holding yourself up to an even tougher standard than someone else would.

Do you have a code of ethics? Are you trying your hardest? Are you working up to your God-given ability? Are you applying the highest standards of business and professional conduct to your career? Does your behavior reflect your true feelings and your true principles? Would you like to be treated by someone else **the way you're treating your least favorite customer?**

There is no doubt that we all stumble and fall short at different times. That's just being human. We must, however, continue to right ourselves and aim high when it comes to this key ingredient called integrity. Integrity can never be measured by how successful a person is (since there are many other variables leading to success, including God-given talent). It is safe to say, however, that a person will not be a long-term success without this great quality. You can fool some people for a while, but sooner or later you'll get caught if you're not totally honest. **Strive to be a person of integrity at all times in every aspect of your life.** People will be drawn to you like a magnet because the quality of integrity is so rare.

Chapter 34

INTERVIEW TECHNIQUE #4 RECOMMENDATIONS

Let's quickly review what's happened so far:

You built trust by identifying concerns your prospects had and addressing them to their satisfaction. (Interview Technique 1).

You then earned the right to advance to the next phase of the sales process by asking your prospects for permission to proceed (Interview Technique 2).

You then asked a lot of questions and listened. This enabled you to gather a lot of pertinent information so that you had a clear picture of exactly what your prospects wanted. You then summarized this in your own words—including a priority of their goals and objectives—so that your prospects concluded that you knew exactly what they wanted (Interview Technique 3).

Now you are ready to tackle the next phase in the sales process: **your recommendations.** While this could conceivably be the easiest aspect of the sales process, since you know your products so well, don't get cocky yet. Somehow you have to determine exactly the right amount of detail to provide your prospects. Generally speaking, **people today want solutions and not ingredients,** and thus they don't want all the information which is probably at your disposal about your product/service. Your prospects' different personalities will also require varying degrees of information. You must discern what amount of detailed information each prospect and situation warrants. That's a judgment call on your part. **It's better to be prepared with more information than you need and then back off and not give them all of it**, than it is to be ill prepared and have your prospects wanting more information which you are not prepared to give them. Your ability to "read" your prospects will come in handy here. What's adequate information in one situation might be too much in another situation and even not enough in a third situation.

The most professional sales presentations **should begin with a written Agenda** outlining exactly what you're going to cover. Why a written Agenda? Because in most instances it will differentiate you from your competition. It also demonstrates professionalism. It allows you to have a specific orderly way of presenting your recommendations. **It takes the guess work out of the interview process**. It helps you to "control" the interview by always steering the conversation back to the Agenda. **There will also be less tendency on your part to "wing it"**. Remember that someone once said that, "Ad libs are for amateurs." Another reason for having a prepared professional proposal, including a written Agenda, is that it will appeal for different reasons to the different types of personalities you will encounter as prospects. "Driver" or "A type" personalities will like it because it's well thought out, it demonstrates efficiency and respect of their time. "Analytical" personalities will like it because it shows you are well organized and efficient and will demonstrate that you are a good planner, a skill they greatly value. "Amiable" personalities will go along with just about anything you suggest, but they should be especially appreciative that you are professional and someone they can rely on and look to for help. It will also encourage them during the decision-making phase since you have your act together. Finally, "Expressive" personalities recognize that a weakness of theirs is detail and follow through. Therefore, they will be impressed with your orderliness and the fact that they can make decisions and you'll take it from there. They don't have to concern themselves with a lot of detail. They will see that as a strength of yours that will greatly benefit them.

After going over the Agenda, **a review of their situation including their goals and objectives is in order.** This is the time, too, to find out if anything has changed since the last time you met. You'll be surprised how often either something has changed, or your prospects have modified their goals and objectives (including their monetary commitment). Now is the time to get that out in the open. **Now you're ready to proceed with your recommendations.** After a short factual presentation of your recommendations, be sure to emphasize the solution your product/service is providing and how they will feel as a result of their buying decision. Anything that you can think of to demonstrate how your product or service, or your follow up and service, is different than other companies and other salespeople will be very valuable during this phase of the interview.

Offering two or more alternatives is also an effective way of making recommendations. Then you will be asking for a commitment for one of them rather than asking for a "yes" or "no" buying decision. Any time you can allow your prospects' choices in the design and implementation of your product or service you will probably gain greater credibility from your prospects. The more they "design" the solution themselves, the more ownership they will have in it and the greater the chances of a successful "close". **Prospects want a "customized" solution to their problem not a "generic" solution.** They are different than other people, so they don't want to know that this is the same one you've recommended to the last eight prospects. **Customize and individualize your presentations for maximum success.**

You have now made some specific product or service recommendations to your prospects. Remember, too, that **your own enthusiasm for your recommendation** being the ideal solution to their problem **will probably do more than any other single ingredient of a successful presentation.** Enthusiasm sells! The next phase of the interview process is asking for the order—better known as "closing".

Chapter 35

"I AM NATURE'S GREATEST MIRACLE"*

> *"There is no such thing as an average man. Each one of us is a unique individual. Each one of us expresses his humanity in some distinctly different way. The beauty and the bloom of each human soul is a thing apart — a separate holy miracle under God, never once repeated throughout all the millenniums of time."*
>
> —Lane Weston

You are unique. Not since the beginning of time has anyone ever been just like you. The expression, "they broke the mold when you were born" isn't true, but it is accurate in concept. No one has your voice, your fingerprints or your handwriting. You walk and talk differently than anyone else who has ever lived. Even "identical" twins are unique and different—different laughs, different cries, different smiles, and different frowns. The list goes on. **You are indeed a miracle of God.** The gift of life is a precious gift from the Master Craftsman.

Your heart pumps more than 600,000 gallons of blood each year through 60,000 miles of veins, arteries and capillaries. As a human being your arms and hands, legs and feet can do more than any other of God's creatures. And your mind? Wow! Your three pound brain contains more than 13 billion nerve cells. It's the most complex computer system ever developed. All others pale in comparison to it. **You have been built for success and engineered for greatness! To top it all off—God created you in His own image.** That's awesome!

Your potential is limitless. As nature's greatest miracle, you're challenged to use your powers, your abilities and your mind to the greatest extent possible. That means you can be creative in your business. You can try lots of different things. Some will work and others won't. That's okay. **You can do things your way because in sales you are not held back by corporate politics, bureaucratic structure or leaders without vision.** You're only held back by your own shortcomings, your own negative agenda and your own feeble attempts.

As nature's greatest miracle you also have a tremendous responsibility. It behooves you to use what God has entrusted to you. Your philosophy might well be that **reaching your full God-given potential is not optional but obligatory.** That's good. Words to live by. Words to remember. While we are created equal in God's sight, we all have different abilities and talents. Let's use them!

Have you ever experienced a time when everything you did seemed to click? You felt you were unbeatable? You felt like you could accomplish almost anything? Athletes sometimes feel that way when they describe themselves as "being in the zone". Everything they do seems to work perfectly. The baseball being pitched to them seems as big as a grapefruit. The basket in basketball appears as big as an ocean. The hole they are putting at on a golf course looks like a peach basket. Whether you are an athlete or not, you have that kind of potential every day of your life. The variable that probably changes is your attitude. **As life's greatest miracle you have the potential to change the world.** Just think what a difference one idea whose time has come can make in the world. You've seen it literally hundreds of times with new products, new innovative ideas and creative solutions. You have the potential to be that kind of an innovator. **Never sell yourself short, for you are indeed nature's greatest miracle.**

* The title of the Scroll Marked IV from Og Mandino's classic best seller *The Greatest Salesman in the World,* Lifetime Books Publisher

Chapter 36

TRADITION

"Ask yourself the famous Peter Drucker question about every activity you examine: 'If we weren't doing this today, would we start doing it now?'"
—Executive Speechwriter Newletter
Volume 9 Number 4

One of my all-time favorite plays is "Fiddler on the Roof." I saw it again recently and found it as poignant as ever. The opening scene and first score is about tradition. There's a great line in it. When Tevya is asked why they do something a certain way, his answer is, "Tradition!". Tevya adds, "Here in Antevya we have traditions for everything." Then a younger man asked how these traditions got started. Everyone leaned forward straining to here Tevya's profound answer. His reply was a classic, "I don't know!"

How many "traditions" are you keeping just because you've always done it that way? We are all creatures of habit. We all tend to do things repetitiously. It's easy to get in a groove and not change. After all, that keeps us in our comfort zone. Instead, **we should periodically question everything we do.** This will cause us to either prove to ourselves that it is worthwhile or else prove that a change is necessary. That's healthy!

Currently, when things are changing so rapidly it's dangerous to stay the same because of tradition. If you continue to do what you've always done, then chances are you may continue to get what you've always gotten. But chances are also good your results just won't be as good anymore. If the competition is changing and improving, then you must too. Just look at giants of the past—IBM, Sears, Motorola and see how their failure to change, their success, has been their undoing. Do the Fortune 500 companies stay the same over a period of a decade? Not likely. The saying "success breeds success" is true to a certain extent because success brings confidence, a good reputation and knowledge. Unfortunately, **the new paradigm is that "success breeds failure" because it also breeds complacency, apathy and "traditions" which prevent changing and improving.**

Do you remember the story of the woman baking a ham who routinely cut about four inches off the end before putting it in the oven? When her husband asked, "Why?", her reply was, "Because my mom always did it that way." When her mother was asked that same question, she, too, said the same thing. "That's the way my mom taught me to do it." When her grandmother was asked why she always cut about four inches off the end of the ham, she said, "So that it would fit in the pan I used."

Are there some "traditions" you're holding on to for no apparent reason? Do you routinely question things you're doing and ask why? Are you constantly innovating and making changes even when things are going well and working? These are all important questions to ask yourself. To continue to succeed in the future in almost any career, requires a commitment to change and a commitment to improvement.

Some traditions are timeless and should never be changed. Like commitment to excellence. And complete customer satisfaction. Like uncompromising integrity and values.

And quality service to your customers. Other traditions will keep you from making the changes you need to make to stay competitive in a rapidly changing marketplace. Avoid these traditions like you would cutting four inches off the end of the ham. **Knowing which traditions are timeless and which are fleeting will be a key to success in the future.** Make sure the traditions you keep are the time honored traditions that transcend trends and do not change with the times. Fifty years ago, most traditions were revered and prestigious. In business today, however, they should be viewed suspiciously, for they may be the death knell of another complacent corporation resting on its laurels. Don't let your success breed failure. **Question your own traditions and make changes and improvements as necessary.** If you do, your traditions will be well founded.

Chapter 37

BUILDING LONG TERM RELATIONSHIPS

"Don't walk in front of me, I may not always follow...Don't walk behind me, I may not always lead...Just walk beside me and be my friend."
—Author Unknown

Most sales careers are based on repeat sales to loyal customers. Building long term relationships, therefore, is not only important but imperative. Here are ten ideas to help you build those long term relationships.

1. **Smile first.** It's pretty hard to be mean to someone who is smiling at you.
2. **Find some common ground.** It's easy to communicate with someone else who has similar interests or concerns. Explore and find them.
3. **Listen more and talk less.** Most people love to talk and love it even more when they find someone willing to listen. Be that someone.
4. **Make people feel important**. Give them reasons to feel good about themselves. Make sure they know they're special.
5. **Be quick to praise**. Concentrate on the positive things, not the negative things. People love to receive compliments. Make sure they're sincere and genuine.
6. **Display positive body language.** Make sure your body is communicating a positive message. A forward lean while listening demonstrates interest. Nodding approval encourages more conversation. An open stance and a warm smile demonstrate warmth, caring and acceptance.

7. **Demonstrate empathy.** Put yourself in the other person's situation and try to imagine exactly how they are feeling.
8. **Be consistent.** Nothing can be more detrimental to a relationship than inconsistency. People like to know exactly where they stand. Your behavior should demonstrate how you are thinking and feeling.
9. **Be sincere and genuine.** You can spot a phony a mile away. Never laugh more raucously than the situation dictates.
10. **Anticipate expectations.** People are different. They have different needs, different goals and different comfort levels. Learn to recognize the "signals" people give so you can anticipate their needs and allow them to stay in their comfort zone.

There you have it. Ten ideas to work on to help you to develop those long term relationships. It's worth the effort. After all, **it's easier and less costly working with satisfied customers than it is to develop new ones.**

Chapter 38

ON RISKING

"Man cannot discover new oceans unless he has the courage to lose sight of the shore."

— Andre Gide
Nobel Prize Winner

One of the biggest challenges facing salespeople is their ability to handle rejection. Salespeople simply have to have thick skin when it comes to rejection. Salespeople have to be willing to lay it on the line every day and risk rejection. That's why a sales career is absolutely the worst career for most people. Most people simply could not do what you do. But that makes it simply a fabulous career for someone who has the ability to get up off the ground after they've been knocked down. **Salespeople simply have to be willing to risk.**

Risk comes in many shapes and sizes. It could be dropping in on "Mr. Big" again and again in order to gain an appointment. It could be going out on a limb and thinking big and recommending the biggest sale you've ever had. It could also mean contacting 15% more people than any other salesperson in the district. **Risking means that you're willing to take a chance on failing.** It also means you're willing to take a calculated gamble on winning, too!

Here's the advice I got from someone early on in my career, "Dick, if you see enough people, sooner or later someone is bound to make a mistake and buy from you." Great advice! Risk a lot! Seeing enough people means being willing to risk more often than the average person. Is it hard work? Of course! Is it rewarding work? You bet! Usually the most successful sales people have risked the most. In other words, the harder they've worked, the luckier they've gotten. Funny how that works! Isn't that great news though? I don't know about you but I sure don't possess the greatest intelligence in the world. But sales success doesn't go to the people with the greatest intelligence. **Success generally goes to the people who work the hardest and risk the most**. That's encouraging. You can do that!

Risking is a state of mind. **It's determination, courage, persistence, hard work, and discipline, all rolled into one.** It's not letting variables which are beyond your control determine your success or failure. Risking is your commitment to see as many people as it takes to be successful. Risking is making more phone calls than the absolute minimum. Risking is making five more stops when you get stood up for an appointment, rather than going back to the office right away. Risking is letting it all hang out in an interview and trying to close just one more time than your customer says, "No". Risking is treading even where angels fear to tread. Risking is setting lofty goals and telling everyone about them. **Risking is asking someone to hold you accountable for your activity level.** Risking is challenging another salesperson to a contest. Risking is asking a "coach" to go with you on interviews to critique you so that you can improve. Risking is trying different marketing techniques to see which is the most effective. Risking is venturing into new market niches. Risking is trying a direct mail campaign that's never been tried before. Risking is investing in your business, advertising, seminar selling and even some other uncharted waters. Risking is aggressively, proactively taking advantage of every opportunity to position yourself in front of prospects and customers. Risking is being persistent when all others have backed off. **Risking is getting out of your comfort zone and staying there for longer periods of time.** Risking is living life intentionally to the maximum!.

What can happen when you risk often? Obviously the down side is that you will fail more often. What does that "cost" you? Usually, not much! No one shot at you. No one took food off your family's table. Probably no one even got upset with you or made you feel badly that you took the risk. Actually, whether you failed or succeeded, you will probably have a great feeling of accomplishment for having made the effort. **At the very least you will probably feel satisfied and content that you gave it your best shot.** And the upside? Wow! The great exhilaration that comes with hard work and success. The great feeling that you get when you "connect" with people. **The thrill that comes with helping people. It doesn't get much better than that!**

Risking. Hard work and a tough job for sure. But it's what sales is all about. If you're not into risking, then you should certainly be looking for a change in careers. **Risking and sales are essentially synonymous.** The downside is tolerable and overrated and the upside is what every salesperson dreams about. Success. Start risking more and watch your "PB" (Personal Best) increase dramatically. **It's worth the risk!**

Chapter 39

WE BELIEVE

"He who floats with the current, who does not guide himself according to higher principles, who has no ideal, no real standards—such a man is a mere article of the world's furniture—a thing moved instead of a living and moving being—an echo, not a voice."
—Henri Frederic Amiel
Swiss Essayist

What values are important to you? What is it that you hold sacred? What specifically strikes at your very core? What exactly do you believe? Have you performed a self-assessment recently to determine what is really important to you? Have you developed a business philosophy? It's worth considering. **Your guiding principles, values and beliefs should help mold every decision you make.** They should make the many choices you face more simple and straightforward. They should take a lot of the guess work out of situations that are perplexing and troublesome. Peer pressure, pressure to succeed, financial pressure and other stresses put added strain on minds already burdened by a checkered history of poor choices and past failures. **Decisions which can be made in advance through a principled belief system will eliminate or minimize choices which could compromise your values and principles.**

Here are some of our Agency's philosophies. We hold them dear and sacred and share them at the risk of coming across as arrogant or vain. We believe in them and try to live up to them.

1. **Attitude:**

    We believe reaching our full God-given potential is not optional but obligatory.

    We believe "Being cheerful keeps you healthy" (Proverbs 17:22).

    We believe that character is what you do when you think no one is looking.

    We believe that no one can make you feel inferior without your consent.

    We believe it's far better to pick someone else up than it is to pull someone else down.

    We believe every business setback can be turned into a profitable learning experience.

    We believe the only failure is when you stop trying.

    We believe that you alone decide how you feel—good or bad.

2. **Culture:**

    We believe that the team is more important than the individual.

    We believe in creating an atmosphere of success and high achievement.

    We believe people like to work with successful people.

    We believe that while this is a serious business, we should never take ourselves too seriously.

    We believe in challenging, realistic, obtainable goals.

    We believe the business should be fun as well as hard work.

    We believe that you have to do it yourself, but you can't do it alone.

    We believe it is easier to be successful when working with positive and creative people.

3. **Education:**
   - We believe "Intelligent people are always eager and ready to learn" (Proverbs 18:15).
   - We believe a continuous plan of study throughout a career is essential for long term success.
   - We believe continued development through all available means of education is important.
   - We believe "It is better—much better—to have wisdom and knowledge than gold and silver" (Proverbs 16:16).

4. **Marketing:**
   - We believe the relationship must be developed before products can be recommended.
   - We believe in order for us to win our clients must win first.
   - We believe people will buy for their reasons, not our reasons.
   - We believe "You make plans, but God directs your actions" (Proverbs 16:9).
   - We believe in listening more than talking.
   - We believe in making it easy for our clients to purchase our products (not making them say, "Yes").
   - We believe our clients are our most important product.

5. **Professionalism:**
   - We believe the professional agent will be honest and ethically above reproach.
   - We believe all agents want to be proud of their Agency, their Company and themselves.
   - We believe professional growth and development is essential to continued success throughout a career.
   - We believe in the admonition from Proverbs: "Plan carefully and you will have plenty" (Proverbs 21:5).

6. **Service:**
   - We believe that our clients expect more than ever before.
   - We believe quality service is the single most important factor in developing a long term relationship with a client.
   - We believe that we must be obsessed with providing quality service to our clients.
   - We believe in delivering better service than we promise and greater service than our clients expect.
   - We believe in treating our clients as we would like to be treated.
   - We believe that quality service breeds client loyalty.
   - We believe that it's not doing 5 things 100% better than our competition; it's doing 100 things 5% better.
   - We believe the quality of our service will differentiate us from our competition.
   - We believe that when a mistake is made we have an exceptional opportunity to demonstrate our caring and our service.
   - We believe when a policy is sold our job is just beginning.
   - We believe we must routinely perform exceptional acts of service.
   - We believe we must be totally responsive to our clients.

7. **Training:**
   - We believe in providing the highest quality training in the financial services industry.
   - We believe "Intelligent people want to learn, but stupid people are satisfied with ignorance" (Proverbs 15:17).
   - We believe in developing people skills as well as product knowledge.
   - We believe "It is better to win control over yourself than over whole cities" (Proverbs 16:32).
   - We believe a lifelong commitment to improving skills and increasing knowledge is essential to success.

We believe "If you listen to advice and are willing to learn, one day you will be wise" (Proverbs 19:20).

8. **Work Ethic:**
   We believe we should all be evaluated by performance not potential.
   We believe that perseverance is the key element of success.
   We believe that hard work is always rewarded.
   We believe "Hard work will give you power; being lazy will make you a slave" (Proverbs 12:24).
   We believe "Genius is one percent inspiration and ninety-nine percent perspiration" (Thomas Edison).
   We believe that a high level of activity, over time, will yield high performance.
   We believe hard work will entitle you to periods of rest and relaxation.

Obviously we take our philosophies and values seriously. We think it tells a lot about who we are and how we operate. **Hopefully it speaks volumes about our character, our commitment to excellence and the culture we are attempting to build.** It's an indication that success doesn"t happen by accident, but intentionally through thorough planning, a good work ethic and dedicated service. In short, **we try to live our lives intentionally.** While we don't claim to live every one of these philosophies every day of our business lives, it's certainly something to keep in front of us and to strive to do. **Nothing is more important than your value system.** It determines everything you do and every decision you make. Develop a business philosophy statement and then practice those beliefs on a daily basis.

Chapter 40

"I WILL LIVE THIS DAY AS IF IT IS MY LAST"*

"I expect to pass through life but once. If, therefore, there be any kindness I can show, or any good thing I can do to any fellow being, let me do it now, as I shall not pass this way again."

—William Penn

You have probably been asked the question at some time during your lifetime, "If you knew this was your last day on earth, what would you do?" It makes for interesting conversation and discussion. Television programs have centered around this theme and it makes for high drama and intriguing episodes.

Realistically, you'll probably never have that insight or advance warning that you are, in fact, living the last day of your life. That's probably more of a blessing than a problem! Rather than thinking fatalistically and waiting for the "ax to fall", you can live your life productively without worry or anxiety about death. As a Christian it's really a win-win situation, isn't it? If you wake up tomorrow, great! Another day the Lord has given to you! If you don't wake up tomorrow, great too! The Lord in His divine wisdom has called you home to a place He has prepared for you. And it's even a better place! Which reminds me of the great discussion two elderly gentlemen were having about whether or not there's baseball in heaven. They made a pact that the first one up there would return one time and let the other person know. Ed went first and a short time later visited Elmer. He said, "Elmer, I have good news and bad news. First, the good news—there is baseball in heaven." Elmer said, "That's great, but what's the bad news?" Ed said, "You're the starting pitcher in tomorrow night's ball game!"

Your days are numbered. Eventually everyone will experience the second of the two inevitable—taxes and death. It is calming to know that God is in charge. You would be wise then, to live this day as if it is your last. **What that means is no holding back.** It means that life is not a dress rehearsal but the real thing. **It means not wasting a moment of the day,** but treasuring every minute as the most precious commodity of all. **It means living life intentionally!** You would do well to use your time so it reflects your values. Saying "I love you" to your spouse and children would be a 'must'. You would also want to concentrate on the important things rather than what seems urgent. Complimenting three people should be fit in somewhere. Slowing down to "smell the roses" seems a natural. Most of all, you would want to be certain that your relationship with Jesus Christ is where it should be.

Have you had a "wake up call" recently? An event that caused you to really take stock of your life and how you were spending your time? That "call" came to me not long ago in the form of cancer. It has made me look at life much differently than before. It has helped me appreciate things I often just took for granted. It has given me a different perspective. If you have had a "wake up call" yourself, then you have probably evaluated your dreams, your goals and your plans for the future. **The future, however, holds no promises (except those**

from above), so live this day as if it is your last. And then with Og Mandino you can conclude, "And if it is not, I shall fall to my knees and give thanks." Either way, you're a winner!

* The title of the Scroll Marked V from Og Mandino's classic best seller, *The Greatest Salesman in the World,* Lifetime Books Publisher

Chapter 41

GOOD ADVICE

"Preparedness is the key to success and victory."
—Douglas MacArthur

You have probably heard the familiar carpenter's advice, **"Measure twice; cut once."** It makes a lot of sense, doesn't it? It reminds me of the adage, "An ounce of prevention is worth a pound of cure." Same message, isn't it? The wisdom is inescapable. It's better to plan wisely in advance than it is to have to correct it later. When a carpenter makes a "cut" it cannot be undone. The length of a piece of wood can be cut smaller, but never enlarged. Once that cut is made it's over. Done. A preventative measure for the carpenter, therefore, is to measure twice — just to be sure — before making a cut.

It occurred to me that the wisdom of the advice is very fitting for everyone in sales. It has many applications. **Taking time to plan is certainly one of them.** When I think of all the time I have wasted by not taking time to plan, it leaves me with sincere regret. Whether it's getting a marketing plan together, or planning my day or year, the time spent at this important task has always been well worth it. It has enabled me to be organized, productive, and has assured me that I'm more focused on my goals and the important and urgent tasks.

A second application of the carpenter's advice is to **slow down a little and do it right the first time.** Too often we do things hurriedly only to have to go back later on and re-do them. While mistakes are always humanly possible, they will be minimized and eliminated by going a little slower the first time. It can be a costly proposition (both of time and money) to correct mistakes that have been made. Whether it's processing applications or filling out orders, it makes sense to take your time and do it right the first time.

A third application can take place during sales interviews. Have you ever spoken too quickly and given a fast response to an objection or question from a customer or prospect? I know I have — and lived to regret it. If we "measure" our words "twice" we will most likely greatly reduce the mistakes made by quick responses. **Slow down, measure your words, allow time for some silence before responding.** If you do, you will most likely reduce your "cutting" remarks.

The fourth application is **the importance of the word "measure"**. As salespeople we should always know our "numbers". How many attempts to get an appointment? How many presentations to get to a "closing attempt"? How many closing attempts to get to a sale? How much will you earn per sale? How many sales do you need to have the income you desire? These are all important "numbers" you need to know and "measure". Maybe there are even more or different ones for your particular business. In order to know those numbers, guess what? You need to "measure" what you are doing. When you know these, you'll not only be able to know if you're on track for your goal, but you'll also be able to analyze how to improve. Remember this sage advice I once heard, **"Measurement always improves performance"**. Be sure you're measuring what you're doing — maybe "measure twice".

"Measure twice; cut once." Great advice for carpenters and for salespeople. **Plan wisely. Take the time to do it right the first time.** "Measure" your words before replying to a customer. **"Measure" your performance and know your numbers.** Good stuff! By applying this advice to your business, you'll have to correct fewer and fewer problems caused by hurrying or lack of proper planning. It's worth the effort! **Remember, "Measure twice; cut once!"**

Chapter 42

DELAYED GRATIFICATION

"Don't give up whatever you are trying to do. Giving up reinforces a sense of incompetence; not giving up gives you a commitment to success."
—George Weinberg

Patience is a lost trait in today's society. We belong to the NOW generation. A society so bent on speed and rapid pace, that few people have the ability to wait for results. **Many people today are emotionally unequipped to deal with lack of immediate success.** They know that perseverance is something to be admired, but they simply can't pull it off. They need to experience success now or they won't compete any longer. They are so used to immediate gratification that they cannot wait for more favorable results. In sales, they push too hard. They pressure people. They work off their own agendas rather than their customers' agenda. They want an answer now! It's their timing or else! Also, they don't follow through with customer expectations. They're on to their next conquest. And service? Wow, that just takes too much time. It's time they could be spending selling someone else.

Success in sales often comes to people who are willing to forego instant short term rewards, for the potential for long term and more rewarding results. Delayed gratification takes emotional maturity. Emotional maturity? A lot has been written recently on the importance of emotional maturity. Some psychologists take the position that it is more important in determining success than intelligence.

Emotional maturity is being able to cope with rejection in sales. It is being able to handle the roller coaster ride of emotions that comes with winning and losing sales. Wide World of Sports used to describe it very well during the introduction to their program when they said, "The thrill of victory and the agony of defeat." **Long term successful salespeople have mastered the ability to control their emotions.** They don't let themselves get "too high" when they experience a good sale, nor do they allow themselves to get "too down" when they endure a defeat. Instead, they treat it as a "learning experience". They have a mature emotional outlook that says, "I can only do so much. There are some variables that I cannot control. As long as I do my part well, then I can feel good about myself." That's what emotional maturity is all about. That's what it takes to keep coming back time after time in sales. That's why so few people are really cut out for sales careers. They simply lack the emotional maturity to be patient and accept delayed gratification.

Have you ever been severely criticized by a spouse or someone else whom you respect a great deal? How did you handle it? Does anxiety lead to a greater effort on your part, or do you fret over matters which helps lead to a self-fulfilling prophecy of failure? Is your normal mode of responding to stress one of fight or flight? Do you depend on instant gratification or will you hang in there in difficult situations and "go the distance"? The answers to these questions will give you a handle on your emotional maturity. They will help you determine if this is an area that really needs some work. Recognizing it as a problem is the first step to doing something constructive about it. Here are several steps you can take to improve yourself in this area:

1. **Become consciously competent in recognizing and analyzing your response to failures, rejections and setbacks.**

2. **Give yourself a short period of time to "dump your bucket" of emotion.** Never on someone else of course! A deep breath will do the trick if it's something as little as rejection on the telephone, whereas a good hard walk or workout may do the trick on something much more significant.

3. **Prayer always works.** While it may not always be the exact answer you're looking for, it gives you an extra opportunity to communicate your thoughts and feelings. It's especially effective communication too, since it's going to the only One who can really do something about it!

4. **Choose to respond positively by downplaying the importance of the event.** Ask yourself, "What's the worst case scenario of the outcome of this event?" My experience has been that no matter how big a sale I lost, it wasn't ever career threatening. (That, by the way, will also take off some of the pressure you no doubt put on yourself when attempting to make a big sale.) That should be reassuring! Chances are you'll still have a roof over your head at night and have enough money for nourishment too. And you'll never face death by a firing squad no matter how big the lost opportunity has been.

5. **Figure out what you can learn from the experience.** Maybe there were variables that were absolutely out of your control. Then again, just maybe there was something you could have done a little bit differently that may have turned it

around. Don't spend too much time on this and beat yourself up mentally. Just learn from the experience. Next time you'll be better prepared.

6. **Get back in the game immediately!** Don't allow the experience to paralyze you. Don't wallow in self pity. No paralysis by analysis. Dust yourself off and have at it.

Emotional maturity can be improved. It is not a stagnant state of affairs. You can use this six step method to improve your outlook and your attitude to events which threaten to destroy you emotionally. This six step method will help you cope with not winning immediately. Remember, **delayed gratification is the best kind**. It takes patience and emotional maturity, but it will lead to long term relationships with your customers as well as long term success in sales and in life.

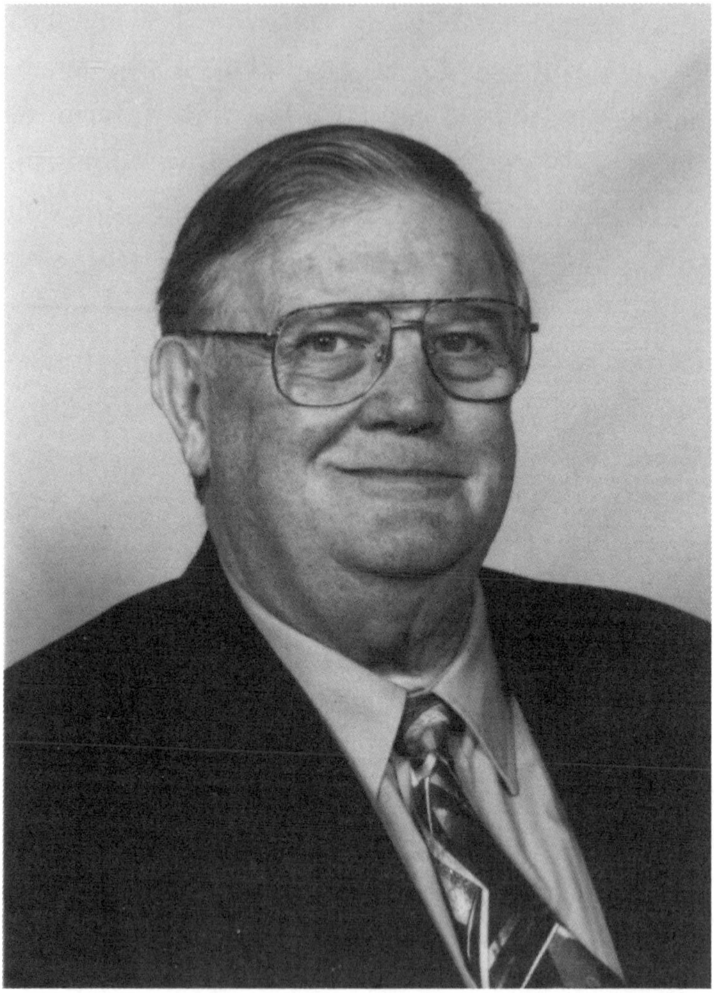

THIS CHAPTER IS DEDICATED TO
MIKE MOSES

Mike Moses is no saint. He'd be the first person to tell you that, too. Yet, this man has dedicated his life to serving his Lord in the teaching ministry. He has been a Lutheran elementary school principal for over 40 years. The love he has for his Lord has been etched on the hearts of the more than 1,000 students that he has taught. While I cannot measure the impact that has had on others, I can tell you the influence it has had on my life.

Mike (Mr. Moses to me then, of course) was my seventh and eighth grade teacher at Bethany Lutheran School in Parma, Ohio. He was the ultimate law in the school. Yet, that strict facade frequently gave way to a tenderness not often demonstrated by a man of his position or stature. His sense of humor in the classroom betrayed his reputation of being a strict disciplinarian. My respect and admiration for Mike has continued to grow over the years. Mike was the third recipient of the Cleveland Lutheran High School Association Outstanding Educator Award. He has received many other awards, honors and recognition. His dedication to providing quality education to the students of Bethany remains as strong and firm today as it has ever been. His service to the Lord in a variety of leadership positions continues even after all these years.

Mike, I want you to know what a positive influence you have had on my life. Thanks for the early prodding, the example of servitude you set, and all the other ways you have impacted my life. Your influence on me today continues for, like God, you're not done with me yet. Thanks! I love you!

Dick

Chapter 43

FAITHFULNESS

"People who are faithful in that which is least wear very radiant crowns. They are the people who are great in little tasks. They are scrupulous in the rutty roads of drudgery. They finish the most obscure bit of work as if it were to be displayed by Him who is the Lord of light and glory. Great souls are those who are faithful in that which is least."

— John Henry Jowett

Faithfulness is a good thing. It is an endearing quality which is becoming quite rare. **Faithfulness embodies loyalty, devotion, steadfastness and persistence.** It means remaining true to your commitment. Faithfulness also means following through and not quitting when things aren't going exactly how you would like them to go. It seems to be in short supply today. Pro athletes follow the almighty dollar and abandon the very teams that gave them a chance in the first place. Sports teams move franchises, all in the pursuit of more money. Greed has taken the place of this great virtue—faithfulness. Loyalty to employees and vice versa to employers is almost a thing of the past. Even customers get into the act by switching suppliers, agents, consultants and salespeople because of small price differentials, higher expectations and little appreciation for past service. Faithfulness is not a trait of trivial pursuit. It should be admired and valued. It should be pursued with fervor and ardor. **Faithfulness is an honorable thing.**

In a sales career it means the following:

1. Loyalty to your company;
2. Commitment to your goal;
3. Never compromising your integrity;
4. Standing by and fighting for your customers;
5. Service that exceeds expectations;
6. Ardent pursuit of converting prospects into customers;
7. Fierce determination in finding solutions to customers' problems;
8. Loyalty to your principles and values.

If you can remain faithful to your company as well as loyal to your customers, you will be set apart as a rare breed indeed!

One of my favorite hymns is written about this word faithfulness. It was written by Thomas Chisholm and it's entitled, "Great is Thy Faithfulness". Thomas Chisholm is an interesting study. He was converted to Christianity in his early twenties when he listened to an Evangelist by the name of Dr. H.C. Morrison. During the rest of his life, Thomas Chisholm spent time as an insurance salesman and a traveling evangelist. Now there's an interesting combination! He wrote many poems and would send them to Dr. William Runyon, a contemporary composer, to put them to music. The beautiful composition, "Great is Thy Faithfulness," is characterized by its stirring tune and its magnificent words and message. It was written in 1923 and is based on this text from Lamentations 3:21-23, "The reason I can still find hope is that I keep this one thing in mind:

the Lord's mercy. We were not completely wiped out. His compassion is never limited. It is new every morning. His faithfulness is great."

Today, loyalty and faithfulness are almost extinct values. Isn't it refreshing to know that God is both changeless and faithful. Read this first verse:

"Great is thy faithfulness", O God my Father,
There is no shadow of turning with thee;
Thou changest not, thy compassions, they fail not;
As thou hast been thou for ever wilt be."
Great is thy faithfulness!
Great is thy faithfulness!"
Morning by morning new mercies I see:
All I have needed thy hand hath provided"
Great is thy faithfulness,"
Lord, unto me!

If you know the tune, I'm sure you're humming it already, if not singing it! If you don't know it, find a George Beverly Shea rendition and you'll be in for a real treat!

Faithfulness reeks of virtue. It takes hard work and commitment. No wonder it is rare today! **Strive for faithfulness in the things that you do. Pursue it constantly.** Don't give in to the trends of the time. Demand more of yourself. Today, faithfulness will subject you to severe ridicule by those around you. Pursue it anyway! Rise above injustices, setbacks, adversity, and ridicule and commit yourself to being faithful. You'll be among the few who have chosen principles and virtues over greed and selfishness.

Chapter 44

INTERVIEW TECHNIQUE #5 CLOSING

More has been written about "closing techniques" than any other phase of the interview process. Super successful salespeople are held in reverence and awe by other salespeople because they seemingly have superior closing skills, or secret closes that only they know. In my estimation nothing is further from the truth. It is true that super successful salespeople have probably mastered the art of closing. But they have just as certainly mastered all the other phases of the sales interview process as well. And, **they have no "secret" closes.** They use the same ones that most salespeople use. **They just do it more often and more effectively.** Closing techniques are very overrated as far as I'm concerned.

Look at it this way. First you built trust with your prospects. Then you listened to them describe exactly what they wanted—their goals and objectives—and then made a product or service recommendation. Closing is simply the next step toward the solution of their problem. Normally, if you don't close a sale, it is because you lacked something in one of the other phases of the sales process. If, for example, you didn't build trust effectively, there is no way that prospects will buy from you; in fact maybe they didn't even give you "good" information during your fact finding. If, on the other hand, you have their trust but they don't feel they have a problem that you're attempting to solve through your products or services, then no matter what you recommend, they will probably balk at your ideas because they don't see a need. Finally, even if you have earned their trust and confidence and established specific needs that they agree upon, if they don't feel that your products or services are the best solution to meet their goals and objectives, it will be difficult at best to get them to make a decision in your favor. **If you have done a good job of establishing trust, learning what their real desires are and have products or services that help them accomplish those desires, then closing will be relatively easy.** As you can see, every phase of the sales process is important.

Having said all that, let's talk about some specific professional closing techniques. A guide to closing techniques is not the aim of this message, but only to give you a couple thoughts and ideas worth trying. Everyone in sales is probably familiar with an **assumptive close where you assume that writing up the order is the next step to meet your prospects' objectives.** You simply start asking questions on your orderform or application. As long as the prospects don't stop you, you'll keep writing it up. You never really ask for a buying decision, you just assume they want to do it.

I like direct closes a little better. I think it's more professional and less manipulative. If you've been up front and forthright with your prospects up to this point, why change now? If you have offered two choices or options, a simple question like, "Based on your situation which of these feels right to you (or looks better, or makes more sense etc.—based on their personalities)?", should work well Another close could be this, "Based on the priorities you have established, it looks to me like this fits the bill perfectly. How do you feel about it (or what do you think about it)?" Here's another favorite,

"Normally, what I do with my customers at this point is fill out the paper work and get the plan going. Are you comfortable with that (or what would you like me to do —with a driver)?" What is really important to remember is that **if you use a direct close, you need to remain absolutely silent after you have asked the closing question.** Whatever is said next must be said by the buyer rather than you. You're either going to get agreement, in which case you made the sale, or disagreement in which case you need to find out why or what your prospects' objections are. **Don't let them off the hook by talking!** It's the most critical time in the interview. **Be quiet!** If you have recommended what is in your prospects' best interests, then you owe it to them to get them to make a buying decision.

Another thing should be said about closing. **Once you have heard a "buying" signal, stop selling.** Once you have gotten agreement that they will purchase your product or service, stop selling. It's over! You won (as did your prospects)! Stop selling! You have everything to lose and nothing to gain by continuing to talk about the product or service. They've already made up their minds, stop selling!

Closing is fun because it's the culmination of the whole sales process. It tells you whether you've been successful or not. It's the bottom line you've been trying to reach. It's sure fun to help people and in the end that's the real bottom line. So sharpen your skills, hone your closing techniques and **close with confidence and enthusiasm like the true professional you are.**

Chapter 45

INDEPENDENCE—BANE OR BLESSING?

"Independent will is the ability to make decisions and choices and to act in accordance with them. It is the ability to act rather than to be acted upon. Empowerment comes from learning how to use this great endowment in the decisions we make every day."
—Stephen Covey

One of the reasons most of us have been drawn to a selling career is the independence that it offers us. Day in and day out we pretty much call our own shots. In most selling careers you need not be concerned about corporate politics, blue or white collar layoffs, the uncertainty of the economy or unemployment. It's not the type of job where you have to punch a clock or where someone else is looking over your shoulder all the time. Just the opposite—it lacks structure, and as you all know, every day is just a little bit different. Most of us not only like it that way, but frankly, we wouldn't want it any other way. Most of us agree with the axiom that, "Variety is the spice of life". We will certainly never get bored in sales! That's the good news.

The bad news, you might say, is that with independence comes responsibility and accountability. **Independence means that you must possess organizational talent and self-discipline in order to be successful.** It means you have to say, "No!" sometimes to family and friends. It means you must say, "No!" sometimes to yourself, too. Self-discipline means making a schedule and sticking to it. Self-discipline means knowing what makes you money and then doing it. **Self-discipline also means knowing the difference between the seemingly urgent tasks and the really important ones and then doing the important ones.** Self-discipline is organizing your "To Do" list with the important tasks first rather than the fun ones or easy ones. **Self-discipline is holding yourself accountable for your results.** It's having a big sale on Monday and working hard the rest of the week rather than coasting. It's buying into the concept that "If it's going to be, it's up to me."

Here are four steps to help you handle independence:

1. **Take time out to reflect and assess how you're doing in the self-discipline department.** Are you making enough phone calls each week? Conducting enough interviews? Asking enough people to purchase your products?

2. **Decide what the important tasks are that you have to do each day to make it a successful day.** Differentiate between important tasks and urgent tasks. Prioritize your "To Do" list.

3. **Initiate a system that will allow you to determine success or failure on a daily basis. It should probably be an activity target rather than a commission target.** Hold yourself accountable. Remember the 11th Commandment for salespeople: "Thou shalt know thy numbers!" Remember that measurement always improves performance.

4. **Plan your work and then work your plan.** Once you've set up a plan don't let other people or things get you off course.

Will there be distractions? You know it! Will you have to alter your plans sometimes? Probably—but do it at your own risk! Will this method stifle your independence? Maybe. **But the alternative may be even more disastrous.** Independence—we love it! Recognize, however, that it can be either a bane or a blessing. **Make sure it's a blessing by exhibiting an extraordinary amount of self-discipline.** It will be your key to a successful selling career.

Chapter 46

HAS THIS COST YOU A SALE RECENTLY?

"The customer is your final inspector."
—Author Unknown

If you've done any of these things lately, it will probably affect your bottom line. Beware!

1. You cut out articles of interest to send to your customers, but you don't mail them.
2. **You forget to write "Thank You" notes after appointments.**
3. **You only call your customers when you need a sale.**
4. You direct all eye contact and your proposal to the "man" of the house since he's probably the decision maker.
5. **Since you're the expert, you tell them exactly what you think they should have** (after all, they have two ears and only one mouth).
6. Your two and one-half hour interview causes them to miss their favorite weekly TV program.
7. You eliminate your 800 number to cut down on phone calls and save a few bucks.
8. You mail your proposals to your customers to save on some time and gas mileage.
9. You flip a coin to determine who pays for the lunch you're having with an important customer.
10. You "pass" on the company optional training session since it's being taught by some home office person who's probably never been on an interview in her life.

11. You decide to just throw everything away that's cluttering your desk—after all, if you haven't needed it yet, you probably never will.
12. **You cut a customer off in mid-sentence during an interview because he's been rambling for about ten minutes.**
13. **You don't call your customer about the shipment being delayed for about ten days since he'll probably get upset.**
14. Right after a prospect just tells his favorite personal story, you pipe up with, "That's nothing! You should have seen what happened to me...."
15. You see a client of yours in the hardware store but avoid his direct eye contact so that you don't get pulled into a conversation.

Make sure everything you do is done intentionally—or it could cost you a sale.

Chapter 47

MARKETING TRENDS

"Those who are always learning are those who can ride the waves of change and who see a changing world as full of opportunities rather than of dangers. They are the ones most likely to be the survivors in a time of discontinuity. They are the enthusiasts and the architects of new ways and forms and ideas."
—Charles Handy

Sales and marketing have gone through a real metamorphosis. Malls are places where:

retired people walk during the winter months (in the north at least);
people go who don't have air-conditioning (in the summer months);
young people gather (mostly non-consumers).

Malls are becoming concrete "ghosttowns".

More and more products are being purchased via catalogues. Mail order businesses are flourishing. The Home Shopping Network and other channels offer the convenience of shopping from your den or kitchen. No threats. No pushy salespeople. No contact with people. No traffic to battle. No parking space needed. It's safe, convenient, non-threatening and quick. It's the shopping of choice for more and more people.

A new marketing system has been gaining momentum over the past several years and is now reaching critical mass. **It's network marketing. It's the wave of the future.** It combines some of the advantages of catalogue shopping, mail order business and TV shopping. **But it's all started through relationships.** People invite their friends and acquaintances to learn about a product (or series of products) that can be purchased wholesale. They are invited to be distributors themselves and even to recruit others to be distributors, too. The products range from health products to Tupperware. From water purifying systems to computers. From candles to pots and pans. The logic of the system is unmistakable. If the "middle men" are cut out of the sales equation, products can be bought and sold much cheaper. Who are these "middle men"? Retailers, stores, managers, and yes, alas, salespeople. Most products actually cost a fraction of what they are sold for in a store. 75% to 150% or more markups from the actual cost to make a product, are not unusual. By eliminating the "middle men" these same products can be purchased much more reasonably. Once you have had a demonstration of the products and learned about the company from a friend or acquaintance, you will be able to make all future purchases from the convenience of your own home —-wholesale! You simply sign up to become a distributor yourself. And if you recruit others to become distributors, you actually receive money based on their purchases and recruits. **It's safe, easy, convenient, quick, and cheaper, too! Wow!**

What threat or opportunity does this present to you (assuming, of course, you are in sales)? Well, **first of all, you better be aware of this trend that is sweeping the country.** Don't ignore this major marketing shift. Second, **you need to find ways to adopt this marketing concept into your sales practice.** Third, **you constantly need to be making the purchases of your customers more convenient and** quicker. Fourth, **you must position yourself as being indispensable.** If purchases of your products can be made without your involvement, they probably will be. Where will that leave you? Your customers better see you as someone they need for advice, service or expertise or they'll take their business somewhere else where it will be much cheaper. You must constantly demonstrate to people why they need <u>you</u> to help them. Consumers today are different than they were twenty years ago. They have different needs and different agendas. They have greater expectations. They have greater demands. **They want speed, efficiency, convenience and safety—at the cheapest price, of course.** What a challenge! Today you must find ways to furnish these things to your customers and at the same time continue to improve the service you are providing them. **Network marketing affords you an opportunity to provide these things to your customers.** Avoid it and sell at your own risk. Rather, find out how to tap into this marketing system for your future success.

Chapter 48

"TODAY I WILL BE MASTER OF MY EMOTIONS"*

"You can't let yourself get on that emotional roller coaster ride over wins and losses. That's why you have to keep an even level of intensity. There are so many deviations in this game. So often you just have to isolate yourself from everything else to try and keep up with your goals."
—Steve Carlton

    The masters are the great ones. Masters are exceptionally gifted people. They have honed their skills and are recognized as experts. They are qualified to practice their craft or art on their own because of their demonstrated experience and ability. They have the power and control. They "call their own shots". They have reputations for being real craftsman and wise beyond their years. To "master" your emotions in a selling occupation is a major accomplishment. **To be able to control your emotions, so they work for you, takes a lot of self-discipline.** Yet, it is essential for long term success and psychological wellness.

    Early in a selling career most people are on an emotional roller coaster ride. A sale of your products or service and you're on top of the world and life is great. One of the real joys of being a sales manager is getting a phone call from a new salesperson who just had to call to tell me about their first sale on their own. They're so excited they just had to tell me about it. Twenty wonderful minutes later I'm as fired up as they are! That's great! Anyone who has ever sold anything can relate to that joy and excitement. If you can't, you're probably in the wrong business. Three days later, however, after a dozen straight, "No" answers to buy their product or service, that same person is in the pits and the hole seems to be getting bigger and bigger by each phone call. Fortunately for most people, the next sale is only a day or two away. With it comes the exhilarating feeling of connecting with people and making that sale.

Your ability to master the emotional peaks and valleys of your career will be one of the determining factors of your ultimate success or failure in a sales career. Here are several recommendations that might help:

1. **Start by accepting the fact that God has given you plenty of ability**—certainly more than you need to be successful in this career.

2. **Always attempt to control the things that you have the ability to control.** That usually equates in selling to your activity level. There are many other variables that enter into this career, many of which you cannot control. Forget those! You cannot control another person saying, "Yes" to you, but you can control how many appointments you have scheduled for the week.

3. **Do not allow another individual the power to influence how you feel about yourself.** Three weeks of no sales in a career does not make you a bad person. Sale or no sale, you're still the same great person you have always been. After the tenth, "No" on the phone, if you can say, "Boy, that's too bad. They could have really used my help!", then you have the stuff of which champions are made.

4. **Remember, despite all your advertising efforts and public relations efforts and your professional marketing approach, it's still somewhat a numbers game.** If someone says "No" to you, they usually are not saying it to you personally. As a matter of fact, in most instances they don't even know you very well. A high level of activity of seeing people, will give you the numbers in order to be successful.

5. **When you do make a sale, rejoice.** You were able to connect with someone. They certainly "bought" you before they bought the product you were selling them. Congratulate yourself. What a thrill! Enjoy it and bask in the good feeling that comes from helping someone else.

6. **Stay focused on your goal.** Determine for yourself that no one can deter you from being successful. The most exciting thing about a sales career is that if you have a good product to sell and sell your product properly, then the more successful you are, the more people you have helped. Concentrate on helping people and you will make your goal.

Each of us has to determine how best to master our emotions. For some it comes easy because they're not very emotional to begin with. Others have to work hard at it. If you're fairly new in a selling career, recognize that the peaks and the valleys tend to level out over time. How quickly that happens will be determined by your ability to master your emotions. Make sure that your actions help determine your thoughts rather than vice versa. Og Mandino put it this way:

"If I feel depressed I will sing.
If I feel sad I will laugh.
If I feel ill I will double my labor.
If I feel fear I will plunge ahead.

If I feel inferior I will wear new garments.
If I feel uncertain I will raise my voice.
If I feel poverty I will think of wealth to come.
If I feel incompetent I will remember past success.
If I feel insignificant I will remember my goals.
Today I will be master of my emotions."

* The title of the Scroll Marked VI from Og Mandino's classic best seller, *The Greatest Salesman in the World,* Lifetime Books Publisher

Chapter 49

AMAZING SERVICE

"I don't know what your destiny will be, but one thing I know: the only ones among you who will be really happy are those who will have sought and found how to serve."
—Albert Schweitzer

A lot has been written about TQM (Total Quality Management) and WCS (World Class Service) in the last few years. It seems like they're the buzzwords of the '90's. They are like "value added service" was a few years back. While I'm a little tired of hearing them, I certainly support the concept of improved customer service. Frankly, if it's been a new concept to anyone hearing these buzzwords they've got a lot of catching up to do. This 'wake up call' for improved service shouldn't be undertaken because someone has indicated this is the way to go. **Improved service to your customers should always be a constant for anyone in sales.** Your customers are your lifeblood. They dictate your success or failure. Anything and everything you can do to earn their confidence, their trust and their satisfaction, deserves top priority. Hopefully you've been doing this for a long time. If the TQM and WCS initiatives have done anything to make that more intentional, then they have been worthwhile.

The goal of every salesperson should be to develop long term relationships with customers. To reach that goal there are two objectives to achieve: **differentiation and positioning.** Differentiation is everything you do which will help your customers decide that you're different than other salespeople. Positioning on the other hand is everything you do to create in the mind of your prospects and customers a positive mental picture of you. Everything you do for your customers should be done with these two things in mind. You want your customers to think of you immediately if they need a product or service that you offer. You never want them to get competitive bids, but be so impressed with you that you have eliminated the competition. No other salesperson should be able to gain entry into your customer base. **Your customers should be so enthralled with your service that no one else even stands a chance.** If you have "positioned" yourself properly and your customers recognize you as being "different" from other salespeople, then you'll be seated in the fabled "cat bird seat". Other salespeople will not stand a chance of winning your customers away from you. **You will have gained a competitive advantage.** If you feel that's a selfish or self-serving goal then you're in the wrong business. You should feel that every customer of yours is better off being with your company and doing business with you than any other company or person in the business. That's called confidence. So while service to customers is time consuming, and doesn't necessarily immediately result in a sale, and can be costly, it is very important to your customers as well as your long term success.

What are the activities or services that you can provide for your customers that will truly impress them and differentiate you from your competitors? **The list is limited only to your imagination and desire to serve your customers.** Sometimes it's a simple thing like acting as a trusted advisor rather than a salesperson. It could be keeping the customer informed from the time the order is taken until the product or service is actually delivered. **It should include asking what the customer expects in terms of service and then providing it. It should certainly include frequent contacts to inform, educate, review, provide service or just to check to see how they are doing.** Customers like to work with friends so if you can gain their trust, their confidence, and become their friend, there's not a great risk that they will dump you and switch companies. You should be willing to go the extra mile for your customers. You should do more than they expect. **Amaze them with your service!** What a hero you will be to them! Then you will have indeed gained a competitive advantage and will have set the stage for a long term relationship. To that end we should all dedicate ourselves!

Chapter 50

TIME TO SACRIFICE THE QUEEN?

"There is no substitute for hard work and effort beyond the call of mere duty. That is what strengthens the soul and enables one's character."
—Walter Camp

Robert Fulghum tells a great story in his book *Maybe (Maybe Not)* about a chess player named Frank Marshall. Marshall was playing a Russian chess master and found his queen under attack. Now if you're a chess player you know that the queen in the most powerful player on the board. Losing it means almost certain defeat. Many spectators saw avenues of escape for the queen and so they gasped when Marshll apparently made a foolish move and left his queen to be captured by no less than three of his opponent's pieces. Upon further study, however, the Russian master and ultimately the spectators grasped the brilliance of the move. No matter which piece captured the queen, Marshall's opponent would be left in a losing position. Marshall, most unorthodoxically, had sacrificed his most powerful offensive weapon, his queen, in order to snatch victory from seeming defeat. The Russian master conceded the game to Marshall.

Frank Marshall was willing to lay it all on the line. He was willing to risk everything. But he did it in a very calculating manner. How about you? How are you doing on your yearly goals? Have you been laying it on the line? Have you been risking like you should? Are you giving yourself every opportunity to be successful? **Is it time to sacrifice your queen?** How many sales are you closing? What percentage is that? I bet you'd be willing to stack that up against Albert Belle's average any day. **Most people don't fail in sales because of the people they don't sell. They fail because of the people they don't see!** Normally the problem lies in the fact that you simply don't give enough people the opportunity to vote on your products or services. If you asked five people to buy your products this week and another salesperson asked fifteen people to buy the same products, who do you think will be more successful? You don't have to be a Rhodes Scholar to figure that one out! Just imagine what results you would have if you just asked two or three more people to buy your products each week? Wow! Is it time to lay it all on the line and sacrifice the queen?

Maybe it's summer when you're reading this and people are on vacation. Maybe it's just before a holiday. Just maybe the economy is headed south and people aren't in buying moods. In all probability, however, some people are knocking the socks off sales records in your company or a competitor's company. So no excuses will do. **They're doing it because they simply made up their minds they were going to do it.** They're probably doing it because they are making more phone calls, providing better service, reviewing more with customers, and doing more of the "extra" things they need to do in order to be successful. **Probably because they're willing to sacrifice their queen.**

What will it take to get you back on track? Stir up your marketing juices. Prepare a one month or two month game plan to get back on track or to finish the year strong. If you've done everything possible, it's hard to imagine that you will not have had a successful month or two. Sacrifice your queen and I think you will probably agree with the saying, **"The harder you work, the luckier you get."** Checkmate!

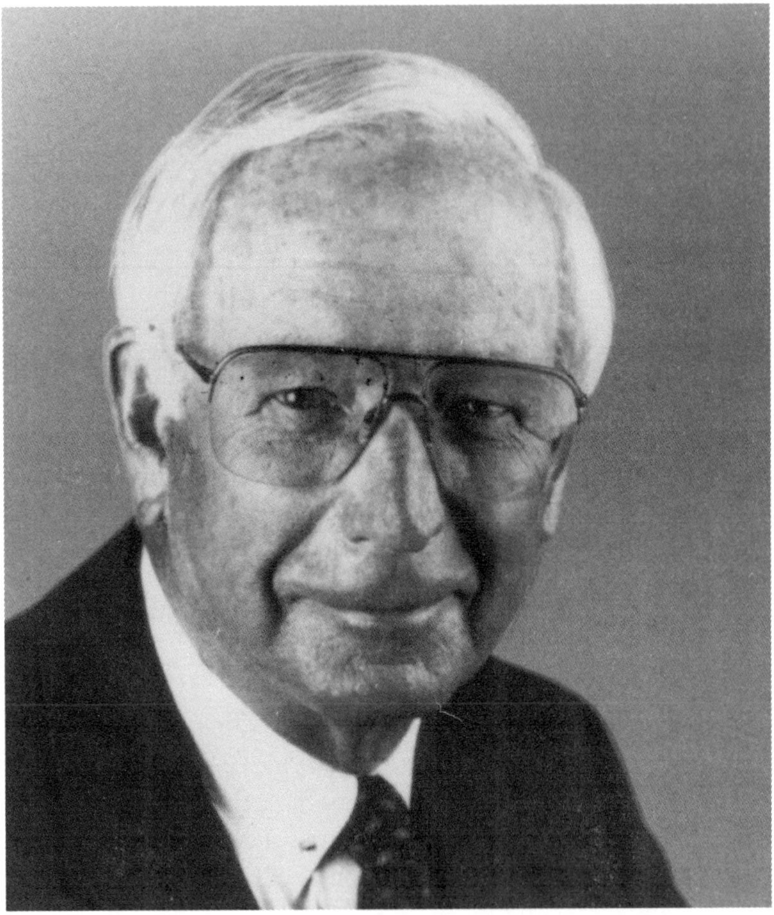

THIS CHAPTER IS DEDICATED TO
CLAIR E. STROMMEN

No one has had more of an impact on Lutheran Brotherhood during the last two decades than Clair Strommen. As a matter of fact, few if any, have influenced the Society in its over 75 year history as Clair has. His feats, accomplishments and ability to overcome adversity during his lifetime have been amazing. He has been a hero to Lutheran Brotherhood! When he retired as Chairman of the Board, he left his imprint on Lutheran Brotherhood in many ways.

Clair was a two sport athlete in high school and college, performing in both basketball and baseball. As a testimony to his accomplishments as an athlete, in 1977 he was inducted into Augsburg's Hall of Fame. After college graduation he had a promising career as a minor league baseball pitcher until fate intervened in the form of tuberculosis. Clair was literally flat on his back in a sanitarium for the better part of three years. Not many people have "wake-up calls" like that; fewer still fully recover and lead "normal" lives. But Clair's life has been anything but normal! He started his 40 year insurance career as a General Agent with Lutheran Brotherhood in 1954, before starting a scratch agency with Central Life Assurance Company. The agency was a charter qualifier for the Master Agency Award and was one of the 100 largest (first year commission) agencies in the United States. Clair became President of Lutheran Brotherhood in 1980 and immediately set Lutheran Brotherhood on a course for its great growth of the '80's and tremendous success in the early '90's.

Clair, the list of your accomplishments and recognitions could go on and on. Suffice it to say you are a living legend. Your accomplishments, however, are overshadowed by your many outstanding traits. First and foremost is your leadership. You lead from the front. You expect a great deal from people and you demand their best. You inspire those around you. Your presence and bearing and ability to invoke confidence are worthy of emulation. Your positive attitude about Lutheran Brotherhood, its people and its future has been a strong influence on all those whose lives you've touched. I have been fortunate to be one of them. Your strong work ethic has set an example for the rest of us and dictated to us what can be accomplished by rolling up your sleeves and working hard. You are a proud person and a competitive person—two other admirable traits.

Clair, you have challenged us, stretched us and made us better. For all you've done for Lutheran Brotherhood, I say thank you. For all you've done for me personally, I say not only thank you, but I also add that you'll never know what a positive impact you have had on my life. Thanks Clair! I love you!

Dick

# Chapter 51

PRESENCE

"Poise is a big factor in a man's success. If I were a young man just starting out, I would talk things over with myself as a friend. I would set out to develop poise—for it can be developed. A man should learn to stand, what to do with his hands, what to do with his feet, look his man straight in the eye, dress well and look well and know he looks well."

—F. Edison White
American Business Man

Presence. Some people say you either have it or you don't. It's self-confidence, bearing, poise. It's remaining calm underfire and being in control of yourself in the midst of a stressful situation. **Presence is being self-assured and being able to impart confidence to others. It's the ability to think on your feet and handle any given situation.** If you've got it, you have one of the most powerful selling attributes you could possess. You have the ability to come across as a sincere sales professional who is knowledgeable, honest and worthy of a customer's trust. We have all been in situations where someone has demonstrated this quality called presence. It's impressive, isn't it? Not long ago I sat on the stage next to the graduation speaker at a local high school. He was deliberate, calm, self-confident and had a tremendous amount of poise. He had presence! His audience was attentive; almost mesmerized by his personality and disposition. There was almost an aura about him. Charisma? He had it!

I'm not ready to concede that this trait cannot be developed. I don't necessarily agree with the opening sentence that you either have it or you don't. We can learn from those who exhibit it. As Yogi Berra once remarked, "You can observe a lot just by watching." **By learning more about it, by seeing it in action, by being aware of its characteristics and by discussing it, we can cultivate it ourselves.** It's worth the effort.

Let's first consider the physical aspects of presence. You don't have to be a physically dominating or intimidating person to maintain a physical presence. **You need to carry yourself well. You need to be deliberate in your movements.** Your exterior expressions need to convey self-assurance and confidence. Your bearing and demeanor should be cool and confident, and almost indifferent to what's going on around you. All your actions should be calculated and slowed down. People with presence follow the adage, "Never let them see you sweat!" **Eye contact is important and people with presence are masters of using it to their advantage.** You should always remain under control. We can even learn from a duck—cool and calm on the surface but paddling like mad under the water.

What verbal aspects do people with presence exhibit? Their tone and their pitch attempt to establish confidence and credibility. **They tend to speak slowly and very deliberately.** They pause and think longer than most people would before answering. They come across as being very sure of themselves. Their answers are direct, most likely more tell-oriented than ask oriented. They stay in charge of the situation or the conversation. They "control" the interview. They speak as one with clout. **They have mastered the use of silence.** They summarize the interview or bring it to a close with authority.

Presence is an intangible quality that's difficult to really get your arms around and determine why someone has it. It can be different things for different people. You know it when you see it. **People with presence come in all sizes and shapes. They have different personalities, backgrounds and social styles.** While a person's reputation, position and popularity play a part in determining a person's presence, it's certainly not limited to those things. Some people might define it as charisma or charm. Others might say that certain people have an aura about them. Whatever you call it, or however you want to define it, it's an admirable quality worth attaining. **The ability to come across to people as confident, knowledgeable and unflappable will elicit a trust** that will enable you to help people reach their goals. Presence....develop it and watch your sales soar!

Chapter 52

OPPORTUNITIES ABOUND

"Opportunities? They are all around us...There is power lying latent everywhere waiting for the observant eye to discover it.
—Orison Swett Marden

Have you ever read the story about the man who worked for the U. S. Patent office back in the 1920's? The story goes that this man went home from work one day very disturbed. He was distraught because he feared his job would soon be eliminated. Not by automation, not by job consolidation, not as a cost reduction program, but rather because he felt all the possible inventions had already taken place. Pretty soon his job would be eliminated because people had thought of every possible new contraption and new idea. As Don Adams would say on the TV program Get Smart, "Missed by that much!" Boy, would he be surprised today! The fact is that the entrepreneurial explosion that has taken place in the last twenty years has caused the U.S. Patent office to add many more workers to its labor force. And, last time I checked, there was no end in sight.

Any applications to your business? Sometimes it's easy to think that the same thing could happen to your business, isn't it? "Everyone has all the _____ they'll ever need." (You fill in the blank—whatever you're selling). "Every possible business owner has been approached about new and improved _____." "I've gone through all my lists of prospects, who will I ever sell to again?" "All my customers have bought as much as I could sell them or they could afford, they'll never need another thing." "My biggest competitor has really wrapped up the market, I'll never be able to break into that market." "I guess I just got into the business too late—all the good prospects are taken." "Where will my business possibly come from in the next year?" Do any of these thoughts sound familiar to you? I hope not. But if they do, don't despair. You're probably in good company. Let's examine their validity.

First, is the fact that **people's needs change all the time.** Families expand, new homes are built, people move, businesses grow and expand, factories modernize and the entrepreneurial spirit causes even more change. The list goes on and on. Conclusion: for most salespeople **there will always be plenty of needs and people to whom you can sell.**

Second, **people have had it with poor service.** We are in a service driven economy and people are tired of not receiving the type of service they want and deserve. Business will continue to go where it is welcomed and appreciated. There are unlimited opportunities in this one area alone. **A simple way to grow in your sales career is to be the one providing the best service in town.** When you develop a reputation like that, you'll be getting plenty of referrals from very satisfied customers.

Third, **people want reliability and guarantees today.** They want to place their business with companies and people they can trust. **They want to work with a salesperson they respect, trust and one who will go the extra mile for**

them. You can be that person of integrity who is Mr. or Ms. Dependable. The person that people can trust beyond a shadow of a doubt.

The list of reasons could probably go on and on but suffice it to say, **yes, there are still some opportunities in your sales career.** Most industries have gone through a real metamorphosis during the last decade. Product changes and enhancements, global marketing, and customer service programs, all point toward more opportunities for salespeople. There are very few careers actually that offer all the opportunities that a sales career offers. Weigh the advantages like **independence, financial opportunities, control of your own destiny, and others,** against the disadvantages. There should be no comparison. If there are, I'd guess it's time to move on. If you are not entirely convinced that you're in a fabulous career, then you should probably begin a career search.

The fact is that opportunities abound in your business. Look for those opportunities in everything you do. Read or re-read Earl Nightingale's famous story "Acres of Diamonds". It's the story of a person who sold his land so he could go to find a fortune, only to find out later that the land he sold had one of the biggest diamond mines ever found. Find the opportunities right where you are! Develop market strategies that give you every opportunity to be successful. Find people who are looking for better service than they are currently receiving. Develop long term relationships with people who are responsible and watch your sales soar over the years as these people become more and more successful. Grow with them. Become a "specialist" and an "expert" in an area in which you would like to concentrate. Take on a consultant role with your customers so they will call you in a minute whenever they have a question in your area of expertise. Sponsor seminars so you can be perceived as a person who provides information and service which is second to none. There are so many things you can be doing that it's probably more of a problem limiting yourself and staying focused than not having enough to do. **Tremendous opportunities abound for salespeople who have a vision for where they want to be and a game plan on how they're going to get there.** No more patents? No more product xyz needed? "Missed by that much!" **Opportunities indeed abound!**

Chapter 53

"I WILL LAUGH AT THE WORLD"*

"Laughter is a tranquilizer with no side effects."
—Arnold Glasow

Terminal seriousness afflicts many people today. They tend to view life pessimistically. They have the "glass is half empty" syndrome. "I'm not a pessimist, just a realist" they'll claim. Yeah, right! They're about as much fun to be around as a dentist during a root canal (apologies to my dentist friends!). The fact is that the single biggest predictor of good physical health is good mental health. **Happy people tend to be healthy people.** In his cassette tape, *"Humor, Risk and Change"* C.W. Metcalf makes this statement, "Our thoughts without medical reservation tend to keep us healthy or make us ill." Does that sound far-fetched? Actually, it's quite Biblical. Solomon said it a long time ago when he wrote, "A joyful heart is good medicine, but depression drains one's strength" (Proverbs 17:22). *Reader's Digest* actually has a column printed each month called "Laughter, the Best Medicine."

Most businesses today are pretty serious stuff. You need to take your work seriously if you are to succeed. Change and all the stress that adds to our lives, only makes things worse. But **let's not take ourselves too seriously.** While it may be no laughing matter, it really doesn't matter too much if you laugh once in a while. **Remember to have fun.** Be willing to laugh and to laugh often. You deserve to have at least one belly laugh every day. Life's too short for anything else.

People with a good sense of humor brighten a room. They make everyone's load a little lighter. Humor can be quite effective in sales situations, too. A well placed pun or funny statement, if well-timed, can be just what's needed if the tension is too great. **Don't underestimate the power of humor in relationships as well as situations.**

Are you having fun? If the answer to that question is, "Yes", then make sure your face knows it! A smile, whether it's while you're talking on the telephone or face to face in an interview, sends a very positive message to the recipient. The message could be, "I like you!" or "I'm a warm and caring person" or "I'm fun to be with (or do business with)". However someone interprets your smile, it can only enhance your relationship. A warm, sincere smile and a sense of humor will greatly help in establishing rapport with someone. If the answer to the question, "Are you having fun?", is "No", then why not take stock of your job and get a career you can love?

One of the conclusions I've come to over the years is that sarcastic, dry and cutting humor can be very damaging. A seemingly innocent, cutting remark may bring laughs and be viewed as funny, but in effect, it can cause ill-feelings, cause others to reciprocate with "one better" and basically have a damaging effect on someone's self-esteem. A good thing to remember is that positive humor is victimless and draws people together, whereas negative humor has a victim and separates people. Be positive!

We all make terrible mistakes now and then and really blow it. Being able to laugh at ourselves and move on is an indication of a good self-worth and an ego that's under control. Laugh and the world will laugh with you, as the saying goes. Yes, you're probably in a serious business, **but don't develop terminal seriousness. Smile, laugh and make it a fun day—life's too short for anything else.**

* The title of the Scroll Marked VII from Og Mandino's classic best seller, *The Greatest Salesman in the World,* Lifetime Books Publisher

Chapter 54

AN INCONVENIENCE ....OR A PROBLEM?

"Little minds are tamed and subdued by misfortune, but great minds rise above it."
— Washington Irving

You have probably heard of the name Robert Fulghum. He has written the best selling books *All I Really Need to Know I Learned in Kindergarten* and *It Was on Fire When I Lay Down on It*. In his more recent book, *Uh-Oh*, he wrote about a man by the name of Sigmund Wollman. Sigmund Wollman, like Victor Frankl, was a Jewish man who survived three years in a Nazi concentration camp at Auschwitz. Robert Fulghum once complained to Wollman about the food they were receiving as employees of a resort inn in the Sierra Nevadas of northern California. Wollman let the harangue go on for about twenty minutes before he finally stopped him and said, "Fulghum, you think you know everything, but you don't know the difference between an inconvenience and a problem. If you break your neck—then you've got a problem. Everything else is inconvenience. Life is inconvenient. Life is lumpy. **Learn to separate the inconveniences from the real problems.** You will live longer." Wow! Great advice! We're all guilty at times of turning molehills into mountains. We let some of the little "inconveniences of life" somehow develop into major league problems. Lee Dreifuss, the former Governor of Wisconsin who does a lot of public speaking, put it this way, "To me, Okinawa was a 10. Everything since then has been a 4." That's putting things into perspective, isn't it?

Do you face problems or inconveniences in your business life? Well, if you think they are problems, think again! If you lost the biggest case you ever worked on what would be the consequences? Not death by a firing squad, that's for certain! If you ever think you have a problem in your business then just ask yourself this simple question, "What's the worst case scenario if this particular event happens or doesn't happen?" That should shed some light on its significance. And chances are you will probably come to the conclusion that it's merely an inconvenience and not a real problem. Robert Fulghum calls this the Wollman Test of Reality. Is it a problem or an inconvenience? Fulghum concludes with these words, "Life is lumpy. And a lump in the oatmeal, a lump in the throat and a lump in the breast are not the same lump. One should learn the difference." Amen!

Can't seem to get enough appointments? Lost a big sale? Having a bad month? One of your better customers canceling a big order? None of these things are obviously pleasant to deal with and they're very frustrating when they occur. But in the "big picture" of life they probably rate no more than a blip and not even a mention in your life history. **So keep things in perspective.** Try the Wollman Test of Reality. Is it a problem or an inconvenience? The difference was sure brought to my attention not long ago when I found out I had cancer. Now, every day is a blessing. Even the more serious events that used to be major concerns are now mere inconveniences. In the big picture of life an awful lot of things are simply inconveniences.

By controlling your attitude toward the inconveniences you will be shaping a better and more successful tomorrow. Yes, life is lumpy. But knowing the difference between lumps will make all the difference in the world.

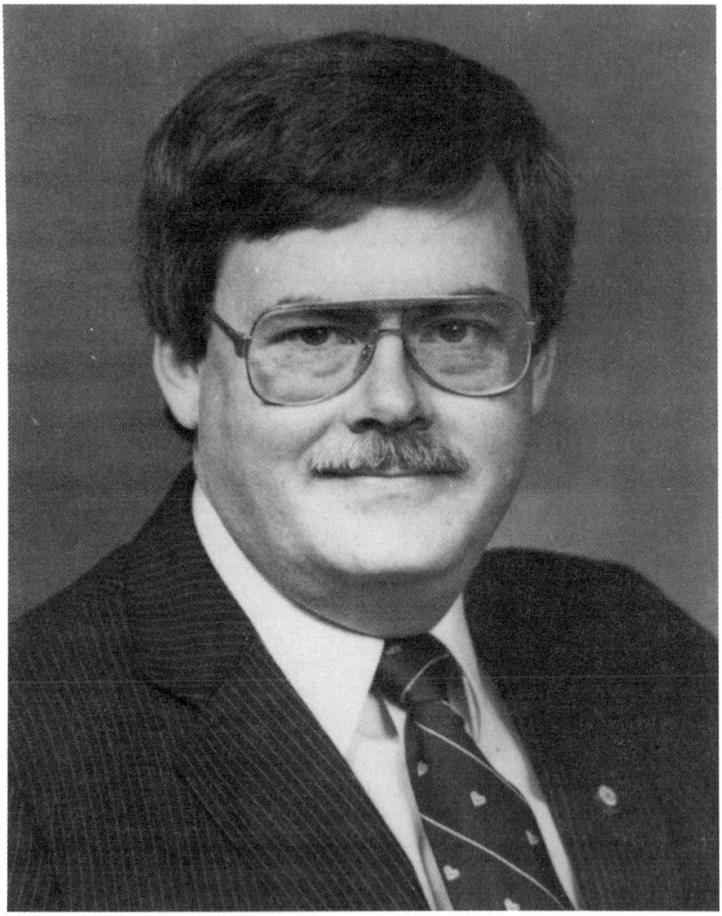

THIS CHAPTER IS DEDICATED TO
JOHN FISH

What do you say about a person who's been your best friend for almost forty years? That's a tough assignment. John and I go all the way back to the 4th grade at Bethany Lutheran School in Parma, Ohio. Outside my family, I have had more fun and shared more of my life with John than any other person. We have experienced together all the ups and downs, peaks and valleys, joys and sorrows that life sends our way. John has been my confidante, my sounding board, my advisor and even occasionally my straight man (although it's usually the other way around!). I am more comfortable with him than anyone else outside my family. I could tell John anything without fear of being judged or criticized.

Our grade school and high school days were full of "normal" events and happenings. Yet, I can't help thinking that things were different somehow for us. It was years of inseparable companionship, jokes, pranks, tricks and always, always the best medicine of all—laughter. We had a ball together! Even our mothers who were very different women became very good friends as a result of our friendship.

For many years we were separated by great distances. Our time together for those years consisted of opportune get-togethers, short visits and events which drew us together. Our friendship never wavered. Actually, it was strengthened by John's wife, Kathy's, presence and our love for her as well. Even our boys have had great times together. When we had the opportunity to return to Cleveland and join the same agency team as John, my only real concern was how it was going to affect our relationship. I did not need to be concerned. John has handled it splendidly. He has accepted our roles, been my biggest supporter and never expected anything in return. He is a well respected, highly principled member of the Agency team who has never once taken advantage of our relationship.

John, we've grown a lot since those early days in Parma. But the loyalty, the trust, the easiness I feel when I am with you and, yes, the love I feel for you remain as strong as ever. You are a man whom I respect tremendously and a person whose opinion I value greatly. You are a man of compassion who cares intensely about his family, his friends, his business associates and clients. I know you would do almost anything for me. You have always been there when I've needed a shoulder to lean on or an ear to bend. Thank you for being such an important part of my life. Thanks for sharing so much of yourself with me. Thanks for your ever present support and loyalty. Thanks for not letting our friendship interfere with our business relationship. I especially want to thank you for loving me the way I know you do. John, I hope you, too, know that I appreciate and love you very much.

Dick

Chapter 55

THANK GOD IT'S WEDNESDAY (TGIW)

"Most people are about as happy as they make up their minds to be."
—Abraham Lincoln

Many people today have the attitude that they can't wait for the weekend—TGIF—Thank God It's Friday. That's too bad. Obviously they don't enjoy their work. Their life is like the poster you've probably seen. The one with the cat hanging on desperately to the limb of a tree with the caption that reads, "Hang on—Friday's coming". In a way I feel sorry for them. Living five days of the week while looking forward to two days. Too bad. My advice to them would be that **life is too short to not work at a job you really enjoy.** Get a life! Find something you really enjoy and pursue it with a passion. Don't get me wrong. I enjoy time off with the best of them. But never to the point where I am constantly thinking all week, "Will Friday ever get here?"

Then there are people who are so driven and hard working that they can't wait for Monday to get here. Let's just skip the weekend and start the week all over again. The TGIM crowd (Thank God It's Monday) is a group of hard driving workaholics. They are so task and goal oriented that work to them is more fun than leisure. Some of them are so organized and driven that even their fun is competitive and structured. You <u>will</u> have fun! That reminds me of something I once heard legendary life insurance salesperson, John Savage, say, "If people say they enjoy working more than playing, then they never learned how to play."

Somewhere between these two extremes there has to be a good balance. All work and no play makes Jack a dull boy, as the saying goes. But all play and no work gives your life no value or meaning. **I vote for TGIW—Thank God It's Wednesday! Learning to have balance in your life is very important to long term success, happiness and quality of life.** Enjoy your work while you're working and enjoy your family, leisure time and avocations during your free time. It's healthy to establish priorities so that your life never gets too far out of balance. If you truly enjoy your work you shouldn't have to worry about "rust out" because you'll want to go to work and do your very best. And if you enjoy your family time and free time, you shouldn't have to worry about "burn out" because you'll look forward to your free time and spending it meaningfully. Overall success in life is winning at both aspects. It means being successful at work as well as being successful off the job.

While sacrifices have to be made periodically to accommodate one area of your life or the other, these should normally be short term. It's been said that no one on their deathbed ever wished they had worked longer or harder; but many people have been unhappy with relationships and wish they had spent more time with people or enjoying themselves more. There's more than a grain of truth in that statement.

So it's TGIW for me. **Wednesday strikes a great balance.** I can enjoy my work and spend meaningful time doing something I truly enjoy. Yet, my family time and my avocations aren't too far away either. I don't need to spend time fretting over whether this week will ever end (although I'm sure we all experience those every now and then). The weekend will be here soon enough. I'll have a chance to recharge my battery. I'll have an opportunity to spend some quality time with those I love the most. **Wednesday. It's a great place to spend one-seventh of your life. But then again, if you're living your life intentionally, aren't they all?!**

Chapter 56

PERSISTENCE

"Consider the postage stamp, my son. It secures success through its ability to stick to one thing till it gets there."
—Josh Billings

It takes many ingredients to be successful in the world of selling. **None may be more important than this one—persistence.** Timing in most sales situations is very important. It almost always belongs to the customer. While we can find some ways to overcome certain objections, many times whether we close or not depends on timing. Sometimes we just have to wait till the timing is right. That's where persistence comes in. **It's staying in touch with customers.** It's calling periodically to find out how things are going. It's checking once in a while to see if anything has changed. It's putting information into your computer so you "remember" when to call back and why you're going to call.

Persistence can simply be described as a raw refusal to quit. It's hanging in there with your customers through thick and thin. One of Winston Churchill's greatest and most memorable speeches was to a graduating class at Harrow School in Harrow, England. It was short. It had a powerful yet simple message. Here it is in its entirety: "Never give in. Never give in. Never, never, never, never—in nothing, great or small, large or petty—never give in except to convictions of honor and great sense." That sums up persistence pretty well, doesn't it?

One of the most underrated qualities of persistence is the ability to keep the big picture in mind at all times. Don't let the little things trip you up. **Keep your focus. Concentrate. Keep your vision on your goal.** Don't let minor setbacks get you off course. While getting stood up for an appointment may be frustrating, in the big scheme of things it's not going to make or break your career. So keep it in perspective and stay focused. Distractions like that could sap your energies, reduce your focus and get you off track.

We have had some great examples of persistence throughout history. Sparky failed every subject in the eighth grade. In high school he flunked Latin, Algebra and English. He never had a date in high school—too scared he'd be turned down. Sparky, by most people's standards, was a loser. But somebody forgot to tell Sparky! He was good at one thing—art. Even in art, however, he got rejected. His high school yearbook editors turned down his cartoons for the yearbook. After high school he wrote letters to Walt Disney and submitted samples of his artwork, but was again rejected. But Sparky persisted and within years he became successful. His Charlie Brown cartoons are now known all over the world. "Sparky" is Charles Schulz and he has been writing his autobiography through his cartoons.

Ever hear of Keri Hulme? She devoted 16 years of her life to the writing of a novel. She spent the next four years submitting the manuscript to many publishers, all of whom rejected her work. Finally, another woman expressed some enthusiasm and they decided to publish it themselves. The first 2,000 copies of *The Bone People* sold out in five weeks with no publicity at all. It later became a best seller when its sales exceeded half a million copies.

A native of Zanesville, Ohio played some semi-pro baseball before becoming a dentist in New York. He hated it. To escape he fished the Delaware River. He tried his hand at writing by submitting fishing stories for outdoor magazines. With money from his wife's family, he published a novel, but it failed. He wrote two more books without any success. At 35 his life was going nowhere. He went out west and wrote a western novel. It was not only rejected, but he was told that he had no future as a writer. He was 40 before he sold his first book. Zane Grey later wrote over 89 books that sold over 50 million copies. Today there are still about a million copies of his books sold every year. Persistence indeed!

My favorite example of persistence is Thomas Edison. He tried over one thousand experiments before he invented the incandescent light in 1879. When someone asked him about all the failures, here's how he responded, "Failures? Not at all. We've learned several thousand things that won't work."

There will always be setbacks. There will always be distractions. There will always be events that could cause you to lose your concentration and focus. "Things" will arise that seem urgent at the time. Don't give in! Never give up! Concentrate. **Maintain your vision. Focus on your goal. Hang in there! The winners persist. The losers don't.** It may be as simple as that.

Chapter 57

HULA HOOPS AND FRISBEES

"Never sacrifice long-term relationships for short-term results. Always think long-term."
—Scott Berghaus
Insurance Agent

The Hula Hoop was an overnight success story. Like many things since then, it caught on in California and the west coast and swept eastward. Once it caught on, it absolutely took the country by storm. It was, in fact, a "craze". In 1958, the Wham-O Manufacturing Company made 20,000 each day and couldn't keep up with the demand. By the fall of that year, over 25 million had been sold by Wham-O and other company imitators. Retail stores couldn't get enough of them to keep in stock. The "craze" was not limited to the United States either, but quickly caught on in other countries. I've read that they were actually banned on the streets of Tokyo for being too dangerous (distracting). Then, as quickly as the Hula Hoop craze had exploded, it plummeted. By the end of the year stores couldn't get rid of them, even at 50 cents a piece. The novelty wore off. The fad was over.

The Frisbee was also made by Wham-O Manufacturing Company. It's history, however, is quite different. Wham-O, a toy maker from San Gabriel, California, purchased the right to produce it from its inventor, Fred Morrison, in 1955. It was first introduced as the Pluto Platter. By 1957, it had gained popularity among college students and sales really took off. It wasn't until 1959 that the generic name we all know as Frisbee was acquired and trademarked by Wham-O. (The Frisbe Baking Company of Bridgeport, Connecticut, made pie plates that were thrown around at Yale University. Fred Morrison took this concept and invented the plastic disc in 1948. Hence the name - Frisbee).

Interest spread from college scenes to sports-minded people everywhere. By early in the 1960's a picnic in the park without a Frisbee was a rare occurrence indeed. Today the plastic flying saucer is still very popular. Dogs have been taught to catch them in their mouths. Competitions exist for games from distance throwing to Frisbee tennis and golf. Americans love their Frisbees. I bet I can find two or three in my garage and maybe one in the trunk of my car even today.

The fact is that Hula Hoops were a fad. They swept across the country like wildfire. They also died out rather quickly. Their coming and going encompassed about a twelve month period. Frisbees, on the other hand, while they started out as a fad, have stood the test of time and have become a classic. Their popularity continues after 40 years.

What are you selling? Is your product or service a fad or a classic? Fads call for far different marketing strategies than more traditional classical products or services. If you're selling a product or service which is a fad, you're probably a reader from California (where most of them have their beginnings) and you'd be at the cutting edge of the craze. Otherwise your timing will be off—like trying to sell Hula Hoops in 1959 rather than in 1958. **Most readers** (including those from California), however, **are selling classics**—products and services that are not going to go out of favor quickly or have a short life span. They may still be on the cutting edge of being new and innovative, but they are not likely to be rejected by customers or prospects six months from now. They aren't likely to be obsolete or have a short "shelf life". Sales of classical products and services call for far different marketing strategies. Your sales practices should always demonstrate that you're in it for the long haul.

Long term relationships are essential when selling classics. You don't have to be too "pushy" or coerce people for an immediate answer. Your product or service will still be as needed and in demand six months from now as it is today. **Everything you do selling "classics" should be done to earn trust and confidence from your customers.** Since it's much harder and costlier to attract new customers than it is to retain old ones, **you should attempt to provide the absolute best service available.** You should constantly find ways to differentiate yourself from your competition. New fads are at best difficult to predict. Selling products and services which are "classics" will enable you to establish long term relationships which should lead to loyal customers and repeat business.

Which would you prefer selling—a fad product or a classic? If you have trouble answering that question then you haven't been on a scavenger hunt lately. Frisbees were easy. It was that darn Hula Hoop that took so long to find.

Chapter 58

COURAGEOUS CONVERSATIONS

"It will generally be found that men who are constantly lamenting their ill luck are only reaping the consequences of their own neglect, mismanagement, and improvidence, or want of application."

—S. Smiles

I love that title. Courageous Conversations. Have you had any lately? Well, to know whether you have or not, you certainly need to know what they are. **Courageous conversations are simply dialogues with someone about a particularly difficult subject.** They can be confrontational and occur with people you know who will never make your Christmas card list. They can materialize with total strangers over situations that have occurred. They can most certainly transpire in a family setting involving both parents and children. They can even take place in a business setting. Case in point—one of your last interviews. You know, the one you thought you had sold until they threw you that monkey business about not being able to afford it. You left without the check, didn't you? Maybe you needed to have a courageous conversation with them. Maybe you needed to risk offending them by trying to show them the results of their decision not to buy your recommendation. Maybe it meant, heaven forbid, confronting them openly. Courageous conversations are difficult. They take strong convictions. They take confidence. They must be used skillfully and thoughtfully. They take chutzpah. True grit. Guts.

What are the benefits of courageous conversations? **You will get right down to the bottom line quicker**. You will come across as a true professional who has the customer's best interests at heart. You will be able to separate the chaff from the wheat. Courageous conversations will not occur until you've sold yourself on what you're recommending. Then and only then, will you have the conviction necessary to push hard for a favorable decision. That will only occur when you have done what is best for your customer 100% of the time. I've read that more than 50% of sales interviews actually end without asking the prospect to buy. Salespeople have not convinced themselves first that what they are recommending is good for the customer.

Let's try another one. Have you had a courageous conversation with yourself lately? That's the kind of conversation that **asks yourself some difficult and confrontational questions**. "Have I been working as hard as I need to, in order to be successful?" "Do I really want to succeed as badly as I let others think I do?" "Have I been willing to work harder in a year that's been a little more difficult than others?" "Would I like the service I'm giving to my customers?" "Have I been a good steward of the most precious of all commodities—time?" " Am I as good a listener as I need to be in order to know exactly what the prospect wants?" "Do I take the time to plan so I can be as effective as I want to be?" Courageous conversations with yourself involve some real soul searching, don't they?

There is no better time to answer these questions than right now. There may be some other questions you would like to add to the list. Your answers to these questions will help you determine if you're on track or if you need to make some adjustments. Either way you'll be a winner. **Don't hesitate to confront yourself with these issues.** And make sure you're being honest with yourself in evaluating how you're doing and where you're headed. You get graded every day in a sales career. **Your activity and the choices you make on a daily basis, are indications of your desire to succeed.** The courageous conversation you have with yourself may be all that you need to get back on track and help you reach your goal.

Chapter 59

ARE YOU INDISPENSABLE?

"What another would have done as well as you, do not do it. What another would have said as well as you, do not say it; written as well, do not write it. Be faithful to that which exists no where but in yourself - and thus make yourself indispensable."
—Andre' Gide

Have you positioned yourself with your customers in order to eliminate competition? That should be a goal of every sales person! Imagine a world of selling without competition! What a great situation! Customers want something, they call you! Not bad! They may not always want what you're selling, but if they do, they're going to buy it from you and no one else.

How do you do that? Chances are pretty good that you've already put into motion a plan to help you accomplish that goal. If you have **built a trusted long term relationship with your customers,** then you're well on your way to accomplishing your mission. In order to be more intentional about it, let's examine the question more thoroughly. **To be indispensable means that people will not do anything without totally relying on your advice and judgment.** They surely wouldn't make a decision without first consulting you. Wow! Wouldn't that be grand! Here's a list of some things you can do to become indispensable to your customers:

1. Do everything as if you were doing it **for yourself.**
2. Never, ever do anything **which will detract from the trust** you have built with your customers.

3. Get your customers to **view you as a consultant** rather than a salesperson.
4. Always **treat them with respect, with concern and with love.**
5. Treat them **like a friend.**
6. Answer all their questions and concerns.
7. Go the extra mile for them.
8. Exceed their service expectations—by a long shot.
9. **Contact them frequently**—especially when you're not going to ask them to buy something.
10. Exercise patience, patience, patience.
11. Always attempt to see things from **their perspective.**
12. Stay abreast of the **latest technology** and product innovations.
13. Remember them in special ways (cards, gifts, articles, etc.) and make them feel important.
14. **Constantly differentiate yourself** from other sales people.
15. Always be **sincere and genuine.**
16. Pay **attention to details** and never let things slip between the cracks.
17. When you make a mistake or really blow something, **admit it**, apologize and make it right.
18. **Stay informed.** Continually upgrade your education. Be professional.
19. **Listen empathetically** and always do things for their benefit.
20. **Make yourself available** to them at all times. Return phone calls promptly.

Becoming indispensable to your customers is a worthy goal. Striving for perfection in providing service and always viewing your relationship from your customers' viewpoint will help you achieve that goal. It's worth the effort!

Chapter 60

DIFFERENTIATION

"There is very little difference between one man and another; but what little there is, is very important. This distinction seems to me to go to the root of the matter."
—William James

One of your main goals during the sales process should be **to differentiate yourself from your competition.** The more you can demonstrate how different you are than other salespeople, the more your prospects and customers will want to do business with you. Under the ideal situation, you will be seen as so "different" that they will never want to do business with anyone else but you. Wow, what control! Is that worth pursuing? I think so too!

Differentiation is incremental. It's probably impossible to be twice as good as the next salesperson. But there are probably many little things that you could do which would differentiate yourself from the next salesperson. Ratchet your differences incrementally to create an impression of indispensability. What are some of these factors that will differentiate you from your competitors?

+Appearance

+Creative First Impressions

+Listening Skills

+Total Integrity

+Interview Techniques

+**Written Agendas**

+Professional Sales Materials

+Impeccable Grammar

+Presentation Skills

+**Packaging Your Presentations**

+Closing Techniques

+**The Process After The Sale**

+Presence

+Product/Service Delivery

+Obtaining Referrals

+**Service**

+Reviews/Repeat Visits

Naturally, some of these factors may feature many opportunities for differentiation. Take service, for instance. There are lots of things you can do which will be different than other salespeople. **The better you know your clients or customers the more innovative you can be in providing service that goes beyond their expectations.** The key is customer intimacy. Harvey Mackay in his book *Swim with the Sharks Without Being Eaten Alive* describes his Mackay 66 where he gets detailed information concerning his customers and their families. It's an excellent resource for information on how to gain the type of customer intimacy needed for differentiating yourself from your competition.

Everything you do should be done to build and nurture long term relationships with your customers. Attempt to develop a list of your own factors so that you are prepared at all times to answer these two critical questions:

Why should anyone want to do business with me?

How am I different than other sales people?

Differentiation is more critical to long term relationship success than any other factor. **Find ways to demonstrate how different you are and watch your relationships solidify and become impregnable.**

Chapter 61

JOE AVERAGE

"With ordinary talent and extraordinary perseverance, all things are attainable."
—Thomas F. Buxton

Do you consider yourself a real genius? The fact is that most of us don't come close to fitting that description. On the contrary, most of us are just ordinary, average people. **Average people, however, can perform extraordinary feats!** I'd bet a month's wages that more extraordinary feats have been accomplished by average, ordinary people than by geniuses. That's a pretty safe bet, by the way, for two reasons. First, there are many more average people than geniuses and, second, you can't really prove it one way or the other. Average people can accomplish great things if they possess a few qualities to go along with their ordinary ability.

First, **a strong desire to succeed.** It's amazing what some people have accomplished who had severe handicaps, simply because they wanted it so badly. It often makes me wonder, "What's holding me back from accomplishing more?" Famous football coach Vince Lombardi expressed it this way, "The difference between a successful person and others is not a lack of strength, not a lack of knowledge, but rather a lack of will." Then there's Abraham Lincoln who considered himself very average and who said this, **"Always bear in mind that your** own resolution to succeed is more important than any other one thing." He should know—he overcame many defeats before being elected President of the United States.

Second is self-discipline. Almost anyone will tell you that you have to possess a certain amount of self-discipline in order to be successful. **People who are self-disciplined have the ability to postpone personal gratification.** They do not give in to themselves. They accomplish what they set out to accomplish. They don't allow themselves the luxury of considering stopping an activity until they have seen it through to completion. Successful people put blinders on and stay focused until they are satisfied with what they have accomplished. **Successful people simply do the things that failures will not do.** Self-discipline can also be disguised as another word—persistence. Successful people are people who simply stay the course until they succeed. They are fanatical when it comes to "hanging in there".

Third, **overcoming adversity.** Everyone who has ever lived on this planet called earth, has had adversity in their lives. **People with ordinary skill and ability become successful by overcoming setbacks and defeats.** You are probably familiar with Victor Frankl, the Austrian Jew, and the tremendous adversities he faced as a prisoner of war at Auschwitz in Nazi Germany. He possessed that most desirable of all qualities—the will to live and the ability to overcome enormous adversities. Defeats? Daily! But he had a reason for living and he would not accept the defeats as a permanent outcome. Vince Lombardi hit the nail on the head when he said, "It's not whether you get knocked down, it's whether you get up." Getting knocked down a certain number of times in our lives is almost a given. That's pretty much going to happen to all of us who experience life. It's whether we get up or not that will ultimately determine our success or failure. Have you been knocked down recently? Too bad, but get over it! **Get up off your knees and get back in the race.**

If you consider yourself average, welcome to the group. **We can all be successful if we have a strong desire to succeed, exercise self-discipline and bounce back from adversity when we experience it.** The good news is that you don't need to be a genius in order to be successful. And remember the words of Abraham Lincoln who once said, "God must have loved the common people, because he made so many of them." Here! Here! Honest Abe!

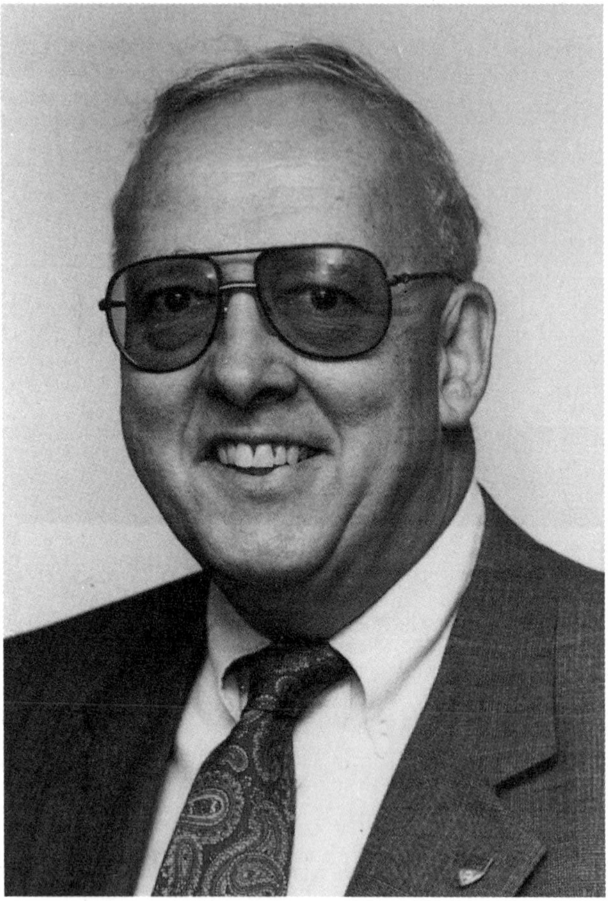

THIS CHAPTER IS DEDICATED TO
GEORGE QUA

George Qua is simply the most remarkable person I have ever known. To know him is to respect him. To know him is to admire him. To know him is to love him. When I find myself busy with seemingly too many balls in the air, all I need to do is think about George and know that he has four times as many balls in the air and doing fine. I have never known any other person so involved and so giving of himself as George Qua. In years past, when Linda and I would receive the Qua's Christmas letter, we would simply shake our heads and wonder how he did it all (and the rest of the family was never far behind either!). He personifies the saying, "Give a busy person something to do and it will get done." He has never said "no" when I've asked him to do something.

George Qua runs Qua Buick car dealership in Cleveland. I got to know him when I was a football coach at West Point. George was in the Army Reserves at the time and a liaison officer for West Point, recruiting in the Cleveland area. He would not only assist in recruiting student athletes for West Point, but he would also graciously supply me with a car whenever I was in Ohio. Our friendship has grown over the years. My admiration for him has continued to increase to where it is today. George, you will never know what a major influence you have been on me. You have encouraged me to be involved. You have inspired me to greater service. You have humbled me with your work ethic. You have challenged me to do more. You have modeled the leadership role for me. No matter what the job or what the challenge, you have always gotten it done.

A typical example of George Qua in action may best describe the type of person he is. One of George's real disappointments in his Army Reserve career (despite the very interesting people, places and assignments, and attainment of the rank of full Colonel) was that he was never able to become a parachutist. By age 61, George was a little on the "old side" by Ft. Benning, Georgia and the U.S. Army standards, so instead, George volunteered and went to Israel and made jumps with the Israeli Army and became a parachutist. That's George Qua!

A list of accomplishments and George's involvement in civic and non-profit organizations would literally take pages to complete. While that would be impressive to those who do not know him, to those of us who do know him, what is impressive is his humility. George takes everything in stride and never gets too impressed by his own contributions. George, thanks for all you've done for me personally. I appreciate your loyalty, your support, your contributions to our community, your commitment to young people and, above all, your friendship. You will always remain the most remarkable person I've ever known. I love you!

Dick

Chapter 62

"NO ONE HAS ENDURANCE LIKE..."

"The answer is simple: if you want something very badly, you can achieve it. It may take patience, very hard work, a real struggle, and a long time, but it can be done."
—Margo Jones

The Chinese bamboo tree is a phenomenon of nature. It's like no other tree with which I am familiar. After you plant a shoot in the soil you will see nothing above the ground for four full years. But in the fifth year it grows eighty feet tall! Wow! What's that have to do with sales? Nothing, really; except that some comparisons can be made to a sales career. Not everyone in this business is an overnight success. There's a thirty year veteran with our company who made 72 calls (actual visits in those days—not telephone calls!) before he made his first appointment. One person in our Agency had a real slump early on in his insurance career and had to sell himself a policy just to get out of it and keep his career going. The list of similar situations and experiences goes on and on. A person I know very well began his sales career on October 1, 1975. After three months he had sold eight policies for $707 in first year commissions. Talk about an inauspicious beginning! Well, more than twenty years later he's still with the company and doing very well. I wasn't exactly an instant success! But, like the others, I hung in there. The sales veterans know:

1. **Timing is everything** and it belongs to the customer.
2. Resiliency to people saying "No" is critical.

3. **High activity** inevitably leads to sales.
4. **Determined persistence** will in the end, win out for you.

I like to play a tape at our Agency meetings. It's sung by Frank Crumit and is entitled, "There's No One With Endurance Like the Man Who Sells Insurance." Don't you love it!

Being impatient for success is admirable and desirable. It motivates you to work hard and maintain a high activity level. Being too impatient, however, exerts pressure on prospects and customers and is self-defeating and undesirable. Sometimes there's a fine line between the two. Case in point: It's Friday and you're at your last selling interview for the week. You sure don't want to be blanked for the week and not turn in any orders at all. Somehow your prospect subtly feels the pressure and backs off from making a decision.

It's very easy to lose track of the big picture. We often let little things sidetrack us from our objectives. We let prospects and customers ruin our mental approach, and all of a sudden we don't maintain the activity level we know we need to have in order to be successful. We lose momentum. Sometimes we just can't see the forest for the trees.

Back to our bamboo tree analogy. What would happen during the first year or two if every few weeks you pulled up the roots to see how they were doing? Wouldn't work, would it? Cramming for an exam in school will sometimes work out all right, but cramming on a farm is unheard of, impractical and will result in failure. So it is in our business. Not everything we want to happen can happen all at once. We must be patient and make sure that we're doing the right things day by day by day. There are some variables that we cannot control in this business, but others over which we have total control. **The variables you can control all have to do with your activity level.** Staying busy with important things like being in front of prospects is how you do it.

Getting a little impatient because things aren't happening quickly enough for you? Good! That's healthy! But remember the bamboo tree. Don't pull up the roots. Don't get too impatient. **Just do the things day in and day out that you know you must do in order to be successful.** As sure as day follows night, success will soon be yours; if not today, then soon. One thing I can guarantee you—you won't have to wait five years to determine your success. Of course, you won't be eighty feet tall either....

Chapter 63

"TODAY I WILL MULTIPLY MY VALUE A HUNDREDFOLD"*

"Success is peace of mind which is a direct result of self-satisfaction in knowing you did your best to become the best that you are capable of becoming."
—John Wooden

Did you ever stop to think what we could accomplish if we didn't allow ourselves to think so small? I'm as guilty as the next person. We build up walls in our minds and they become insurmountable. **Our own fears keep us from accomplishing all that we could accomplish.** We limit our potential by striving for goals that are at best, mediocre.

Medical research tells us that we are using a small fraction of our brain's potential. We have the greatest computer ever built and yet we don't operate it at its full capacity. What a shame! It's like driving a Porsche at 25 mph. We sell ourselves short. We don't give ourselves enough credit. We lack the courage of our convictions. We're engineered for greatness and yet we're not firing on all cylinders. It's not only a tragic loss, but an insult to our Creator.

It's very easy to stay in our comfort zone. Afterall, then we will not fail as often. So we stop striving to be the very best we're capable of being. **The fact is that we're all probably just beginning to scratch the surface of what our potential could be.** Just imagine what life could be like if we had no restrictions, no worries, no fears and nothing holding us back. Wow! **We all must learn to dream bigger dreams.** We all must learn to ask our Heavenly Father for big success and then pay the price to achieve it. For those of you in business for yourselves, just imagine putting your three best months back-to-back-to-back and then multiplying that by four. And that's not even your full potential! What a year it would be!

God can do great things through you and through me. Og Mandino put it this way, "Today I will multiply my value a hundredfold. I will commit not the terrible crime of aiming too low. I will do the work that a failure will not do. **I will always let my reach exceed my grasp.**" I love that last line. " I will always let my reach exceed my grasp." That's great! That's challenging! That's making ourselves stretch and giving God a chance to accomplish mighty things through us. The funny thing is what's the worst that can happen? We work real hard to accomplish this tremendous goal and we fall a little short? We will be much better off doing that than accomplishing a less challenging goal. Remember, if we aim for the moon and fall short, we'll still be among the stars!

Let's work on our dreams. **Let's dream big dreams—dreams of which we can be proud.** Let's challenge ourselves to be the people God intended us to be. And if we work hard and fall short—so be it, at least we tried. Give it your absolute best shot and watch as you multiply your value a hundredfold.

* The title of the Scroll Marked VIII from Og Mandino's classic best seller *The Greatest Salesman in the World,* Lifetime Books Publisher

Chapter 64

JUST DO IT!

> *"Just do a thing and don't talk about it. This is the great secret of success."*
>
> — Sarah Grand

The Nike commercial has said it very well for many years —**"Just do it!"** Bo Jackson or no Bo Jackson, the philosophy is sound. Don't talk about it. Don't think about it very long. Don't even brag about it. **"Just do it!"** This philosophy is not diametrically opposed to the saying, "Don't just do something, sit there!" There's a time and place for everything. Dreaming and planning fall under the "Important but not Urgent" category which Stephen Covey talks about in his book, *First Things First*. You have to be able to determine the difference in activities and their priorities. **Without action nothing can be accomplished.** There comes a time when all the thinking, all the scheming, and all the planning must stop and activity must begin. Then it's time to **"Just do it!"**

Many of the chapters in this book touch on the power of positive thinking. Staying positive in a sales career is essential for long term success. We are constantly bombarded with negative messages via the press and other forms of communications. Prospects and customers say, "No" to you often enough to make you discouraged, unless you're able to maintain a positive attitude. So there should be no doubt in your mind how important it is to remain positive and maintain an attitude of optimism. **Remaining positive is paramount to your success.** Being positive, however, is just the beginning. **Action must surely follow in order for progress to result.**

Activity will fuel your course and launch the attainment of your goal. The German writer Goethe expressed it very well in his essay entitled "The Power of Commitment" when he wrote, "Are you in earnest? Seek this very minute, whatever you can do, or dream you can; begin it! Boldness has genius, power and magic in it. Only engage and the mind grows heated; begin and then the task will be completed." Perhaps if he were living today he'd be an ad man for Nike. Not! The point is that unless there is action there will be no accomplishment. **You simply cannot have a good week of sales without seeing the people.** All the positive attitude in the world does not equate to sales results. Sales only come with the activity of "seeing the people". All the positive attitude and good intentions in the world will not make up for inactivity. **Just do it!**

The business of sales can be difficult for a couple of very good reasons:

1. **You have to psychologically handle people saying, "No" to you** and,

2. **You have to be self-disciplined and a good time manager.** It's very easy to fool yourself that you're working hard in this business. **Putting in long hours does not necessarily equate to working hard.** Reading the mail, studying your products, preparing for interviews, and reading trade journals, all need to be done. On the surface they could also appear to be "Urgent" things to do, but they are certainly not "Important and Urgent". There are a ton of activities in the business of sales that can occupy your time, keep you busy and

fool you into thinking that you're working hard. The fact remains, however, that **there are two and only two activities that you need to concern yourself with** in this business, week in and week out in order to be successful. Those two activities, of course, are:

1. **Seeing people, and**
2. **Attempting to see people (telemarketing mostly).**

Everything else is a distant third. Everything else pales in comparison to these two activities.

So how do you "Just do it"? The best way is probably to establish some built in self-discipline that holds you accountable to yourself. Make out a weekly schedule (yes, that's right, plan!) and fill in exactly when you will be phone calling for appointments. You should plan on two or three short phone sessions per day, rather than one gigantic phone session for the week. (Remember: Life's a cinch by the inch, but hard by the yard!) Then when your scheduled phone call time comes—**"Just do it!" Get started!** Which is your hardest phone call—the fifth or sixth one or the first one? **I suggest it's your first one. The hard part seems to be getting started.** Set an alarm for the time to begin and then when it goes off—START! Set some goals for yourself. Reward yourself when you reach them. A career in sales is mostly a mental game. Find out exactly what works for you. Stay motivated and plan your work.

Whatever your system, find something that will help you get started. That's the hardest part. Remember: "Boldness has genius, power and magic in it... begin it and then the task will be completed." When you **"Just do it!"** you'll be surprised how things will fall into place, because the harder you work, the luckier you'll get. And it's pretty easy to remain positive when things are going well. **"JUST DO IT!"**

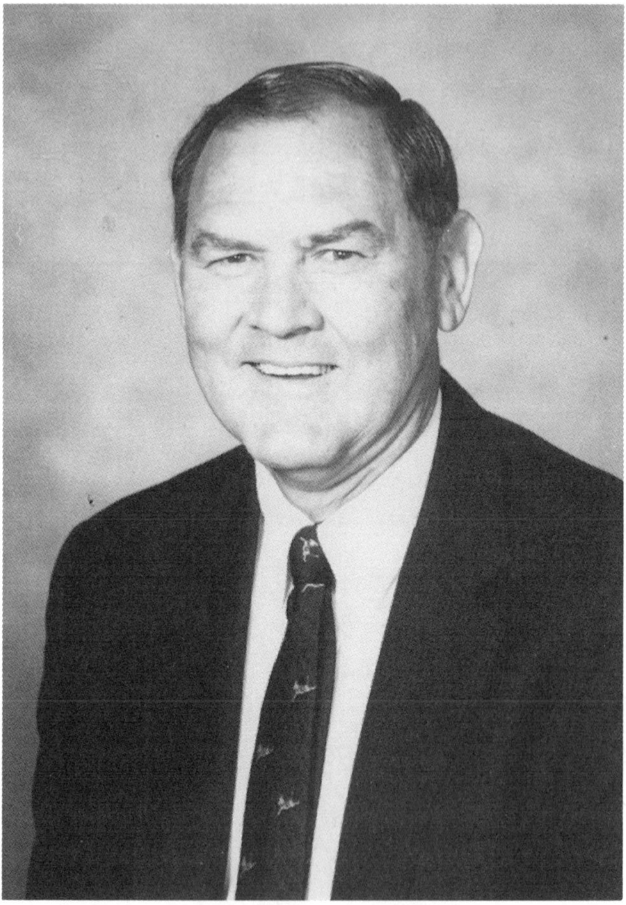

THIS CHAPTER IS DEDICATED TO
JACK HECKER

If you knew Jack Hecker like I do, just the mention of his name would make you smile. Jack's the original prankster and joker. He never really grew up. Basically, he's never had a real job! You see, he's still coaching football. Here's a guy who once commented to a hot shot high school football player who was interested in marine biology, "Well, I guess Coach Yarnell has told you West Point has one of the best marine biology programs in the country." This is Army kid-not Navy! The funny thing is, when he said it with a straight face (while kicking Coach Yarnell under the table), the recruited football player quickly replied, "Yes, I know it does!" Jack is the same guy who calls our office and announces that Bill Clinton is on the line, or Bill Belichik, or Bill Bradley, or Bill Cosby for that matter!

Jack was a varsity coach at Army when I was a cadet playing football. He was an offensive coach and I was a defensive player, so I can't say that I was greatly influenced by him as a player. I was fortunate, however, to coach at West Point with Jack and I assisted him in recruiting football players from the state of Ohio. What a trip that was! Jack has tremendous recruiting skills. He taught me a lot. He once told a football athlete in the Cincinnati area (before he knew what school we were from!), "We'll pay you $500 a month and we'll even get you a new suit!" Boy, did his eyes light up! Of course, Jack wasn't kidding-we got him a whole new wardrobe!

Jack, I have an awful lot of respect for you. You have had a major influence on my life. Your desire to win, your intensity, your devotion to your players, your love of family, your sense of humor, your commitment to your profession (and anyone who thinks that coaching is a piece of cake is sadly mistaken), and your personal pride have all been positive influences that have affected me. Jack, it was a privilege to coach with you, but it is more of a privilege to call you my friend. Thanks for the positive influence you have been in my life. I love you!

Dick

Chapter 63

CUSTOMIZE AND PERSONALIZE

"Don't tell people 'This is what everyone is buying.' Rather, say, 'Here's my recommendation based on your unique situation.'"

—Bill Fecht
Insurance Executive

It's been reported that in a short period of time racks of suits hanging in a clothing store will be as obsolete as typewriters in an office. Soon you'll be able to enter a clothier and have a machine scan your body which will enable you to buy a customized tailored suit exactly to your particular dimensions and proportions. No more searching for a 50 extra long (from which there are usually few to choose)! Tailored suits for your own specific build! Wow!

We can all learn a lesson from this latest trend in fashion. Everyone today wants their own custom model. No more one size fits all. No more generic versions of anything. **Personalize and customize are the orders of the day!** Whether it's a computer system you're building or a financial product designed for a person's retirement, customize and personalize.

Customers today want and demand more than ever before. They want to be treated like the unique individuals they are. We've known for years that everyone has different fingerprints and voice patterns and personalities. In the same way, **every customer has different interests, motivation and other variables which will affect their reasons for purchasing a particular product or service.** Today people want things which are prepared (built, designed, etc.) for them and them alone. Until recently, building and designing products and services for each individual was out of the question. We simply did not have the capability (technologically or financially) to pull it off. Today, however, computers, robotics and other technological improvements enable us to customize and personalize. What a breakthrough!

Can you apply this trend to your products or service? You better! **Find ways to personalize every sales presentation.** "Tailor" your product or service to your prospect's situation and needs. How do you do that? By getting your prospects more involved. **By asking them more questions.** By getting them to describe what their ideas of the ideal solution to their problem would be. By finding out exactly what they want. By asking them exactly what they're looking for in a _____ (you fill in the product or service). Give them as many options as possible. Let them design their own product or service as much as possible. Then use technology to customize and personalize

Count how many ways you are customizing and personalizing your presentations. Start adding more. It will take more investigating. It will take more information. And it will definitely take more time. But if the end result is closing more cases successfully, it will be worth the extra effort. **Add one new wrinkle each week for the next six weeks and evaluate the impact it has on your presentations.** Chances are you will discover that people like it when it's their solution. They will like it when it's unique to them and them alone. Customize and personalize your way to successful selling!

Chapter 66

TEN STEPS FOR BETTER LISTENING

"As you learn to listen deeply to other people, you will discover tremendous differences in perception."
—Stephen Covey

1. **Listen with your whole body.** Let your body language demonstrate your interest and concern. Eye contact is most important.

2. **Take notes.** That will impress your clients and show them that you value what they are saying.

3. **Encourage your clients to talk more.** A nod, a simple "Uh-huh", and even a gesture, will all gently nudge your clients to talk even more.

4. **Use silence effectively.** Remaining silent when your customers are finished speaking will encourage your customers to talk even more. It will also give them the impression that they must have said something important because you have to think about your response for so long. Great!

5. **Ask follow up questions.** This may get you from a "pat" response to the real meat of the matter. It will take them from their head to their heart (an important 18 inches)

6. **Don't allow yourself the luxury of thinking of your response while your clients are talking.** Be thinking only of what is being said and your clients' frame of reference.

7. **Remove**, if possible, **all potential distractions.** This will make it easier for you to give your clients your undivided attention.

8. **Summarize in your own words what you heard.** Ask for agreement that what you said was a good summary of your customer's position.

9. **Listen for what isn't said** as much as what is being said. Read between the lines and ask some in depth questions.

10. **Answer a question with a question** rather than guessing where your clients are coming from. That way you will not back yourself into a corner, but better know how to answer. As an example: "That's an interesting question, why is that important to you?"

Listening is an underrated skill. We all have the opportunity to improve in this important area of selling. While most of us love to talk and make presentations, listening is tough work. **Remember, listening is a learned skill and as such can be improved.**

Work hard at listening — it will pay huge dividends.

Chapter 67

A LESSON IN BREVITY

"I realize I am all that stands between you and the cocktail hour so I will make this brief..."
— Executive Speechwriter Newsletter
Volume 9 Number 4

There was a custom among some African tribes that when people rose to speak, they had to stand on one foot while delivering their oration. The moment their other foot touched the ground, the speech had to end or the speaker was forcibly silenced. I wish some speakers I've heard had to deliver their speeches that way! It's probably something to remember during interviews. **Talk less; listen more!** Try it; you'll like it! So will your customers! Of course you'll look rather odd standing on one foot...

Chapter 68

SOLUTIONS NOT INGREDIENTS

"Time and speed are the currencies of the future."
—Author Unknown

Ever notice that when you go into a grocery store these days you buy **solutions not ingredients?** Ingredients for most people are a thing of the past! We live in a microwave age. We don't have time to bake. We have time to heat. We don't have time to cook. We have time to zap! The pace of life today is hectic and getting crazier day by day. Time is of the essence and baking and cooking consume way too much time for most families. Too bad. Cooking ingredients can prove to be much healthier than heating solutions.

The lesson for us in sales today must be clear and unmistakable. **People today don't want to spend an enormous amount of time visiting with a salesperson.** Hope that doesn't hurt your feelings or come as a complete surprise for that matter! They, too, want solutions not ingredients from a salesperson. **They want someone they can trust. They want someone who knows their products. They want someone with integrity.** They don't want hidden agendas. They don't want someone who is going to waste their time. They want someone who will get to know them. They want someone who can educate them quickly about their product or service so they can make a good buying decision. So we must first and foremost be sensitive to their time schedules. **Time is a valuable commodity these days.** And people guard their time cautiously. People today are also used to half hour comedy shows and one hour television programs. Too much longer and we will lose them for sure. We must be careful in our presentations not to give too much detail. Too much detail to someone who is already drowning in information may cause them to postpone making a decision. Or worse yet, tell you, "No!" Remember this too, **it is much easier to educate a customer than it is a prospect.** If you establish trust and earn a prospect's confidence at the beginning of a relationship and sell something, you're probably going to end up with a long term customer. Educate them slowly over time rather than with your first couple of meetings. Of course that will vary by the type of product or service you are selling.

Have you had any marathon appointments lately? Try to keep them to a minimum. **People want speed. People want instant answers. People want solutions, not ingredients.**

Chapter 69

"WHAT DO YOU EXPECT?"

"It is a funny thing about life; if you refuse to accept anything but the best, you very often get it."
—Somerset Maugham

I'm not a psychologist. Of course you already know that. But I have done my share of studying people. Whether that gives me the ability to diagnose people correctly, you be the judge. At the very least, I'm entitled to my opinions. We've all heard the expression, "There are only two kinds of people in this world...". You can fill in your own, but here are some I've heard:

"The haves and the have nots;"

"Those who make things happen and those who watch things happen" (and some would add—those who don't even have a clue what's happening!);

"Those who think the glass is half empty and those who think the glass is half full;"

"The doers and the don't-ers;"

"Optimists and pessimists;"

"The outer directed and the inner directed;"

"The good, the bad and the ugly" (oh, no—that was a movie);

"The introverts and the extroverts;"

"Leaders and followers."

You get the idea. I'm going to suggest an addition to the list. **"Those who expect a lot of themselves and those who don't."** I agree with the analysis that **you pretty much get in life what you expect.** Some people don't expect a lot in life and they generally get it. Others expect a whole lot and they, too, get it. Are you "getting it"? Life can become a self-fulfilling prophecy. Psychologists have told us that for a long time. They get no argument from me. Have you ever heard any of these before?

> "I usually get a headache about 8 o'clock. What time is it now, quarter to?"

> "Oh, that's just my luck."

> "What do you expect, I'm a middle child."

> "My dad told me I would never amount to anything. I guess he was right!"

Never mind what your dad expected, how about you? Apparently you agreed with his assessment (expectation)! Stop polluting your mind! Give yourself a mental enema! Don't give yourself reasons for not accomplishing great things. Accomplish them! Prove others wrong! Prove to yourself that you can accomplish great things.

Expecting a lot of yourself these days? Or have you gotten comfortable? Has the old surge of adrenaline that used to push you toward your goals been rather latent lately? Has the passion for achieving you once felt subsided? What exactly do you expect?

At the least you should expect from yourself your very best effort. Others may have greater ability and skill, but no one should have more determination, resolve, fortitude and tenacity than you. **Expect your best effort every day!**

You have been endowed with the capacity to learn. Imagine what you could accomplish if you launched a learning campaign. How good could you get? Have you been settling for something less than your best? **As a human being you have the ability to change.** You can adapt, you can learn, you can improve. Take advantage of that! Start expecting more of yourself. **Start expecting your very best.** Start demanding your best effort. If that's not good enough, so be it. At least you gave it your best shot.

There are only two types of people in this world, those who expect a lot of themselves and get it and those who don't and get it. **What do you expect?**

Chapter 70

INTERVIEW TECHNIQUE #6 FOLLOW-UP

Follow-up is everything that takes place once an order is taken until the product or service is actually delivered or rendered. It's probably not so much an interview technique as it is a process of solidifying the sale and your relationship with your customers. It's mentioned here, however, because it immediately follows a successful "close." It's also frequently overlooked by most salespeople. It comes prior to actually providing service to your customers. It is an important time because a number of things could happen which could upset your apple cart and jeopardize your relationship with your customers. **The very first thing which should be done is immediately sending a "Thank You" note to your customers.** This will do three things:

1. Give you an opportunity to genuinely thank your customers for the order (and for their trust and confidence in you);
2. **Differentiate yourself from your competition** (because many competitors won't send one);
3. Hopefully **overcome any buyer's remorse** (regrets that they made the decision they did) which may have crept into your customers' minds.

Send this note without fail a day after your sale! I have never experienced anything but a good reception after sending a "Thank You" note. People appreciate gratitude and very few salespeople express it anymore.

The next part of follow-up is more difficult to describe because it will vary by product and service. The important thing is **to stay in contact with your customers until they actually receive the product or service** you sold them. In the insurance industry it's staying in contact during the underwriting of the contract. Maybe a phone call in a week or so to let them know the Home Office received everything, or they're waiting for a report from the customer's doctor, or "Just called to let you know your policy has been approved. I should have it in about a week and I'll give you a call then to set up a time to go over it with you." In computer sales it might be a phone call to let them know everything is in order and it should be shipped in seven days.

The point is to be in touch with them to keep them abreast of everything that's going on. People appreciate that. They know there's nothing in it for you (although there really is—a satisfied customer!). Not many salespeople are very good at this part of building a long term relationship with their customers. It's detail stuff! Most sales people are already on to their next conquest and have already forgotten about last week's sale. Avoid the temptation to do that. Take care of your customers and they'll take care of you.

The other aspect of good follow-up relates to the different types of personalities. **This aspect is hardly ever addressed by other salespeople and represents a real opportunity to differentiate yourself from other**

salespeople. Attention to detail is critical from the analytical's perspective, so you will be "making points" with this group of people. Drivers may expect it, but you will at least be meeting their expectations rather than disappointing them. Amiables will be glad you're in charge and are on top of it. And expressives will have already forgotten they bought something from you! Not really! But they too, will appreciate the fact that you're taking care of the details because it's something they have no desire to do. They'd rather purchase from someone who will take care of all those "things" for them. So all four personality types will probably appreciate your follow-up—but for different reasons.

Follow-up. It's a great opportunity to differentiate yourself. It's a great opportunity to demonstrate the kind of service you're going to provide your customers. **It's a great opportunity to appeal to customers of all personalities.** Solidify the sale by providing great follow up!

Chapter 71

IMAGE PROBLEM?

"I love signing autographs. I'll sign anything but veal cutlets. My ball-point pen skips on veal cutlets."
—Casey Stengel

Has anyone asked for your autograph lately? Me neither! Isn't it interesting—athletes are revered and adored by fans galore, no matter what kind of lifestyles they live and what their personalities are like. Politicians are well known and receive polite recognition wherever they go. Astronauts command celebrity status wherever they show up. Many other occupations command the respect of people everywhere. Doctors, clergy, teachers, accountants and, yes, attorneys, are but a few of the occupations that people respect and admire. And then there's salespeople! I've seen a list where salespeople ranked next to drug dealers and prostitutes in a survey of "Occupations Least Respected". And I'm not exactly sure what the order was! Sounds like a David Letterman type of list, doesn't it?

Are you having an image crisis? Feeling sorry for yourself? Don't!! Chances are **if you are treating people properly, you're changing people's opinions about salespeople one by one.** It's interesting to note that in the survey mentioned above, most people rated other salespeople as not being respectable whereas they rated their own salesperson much higher. The fact is that you can't rely on other people for your own self-esteem. **You need to believe in yourself and the valuable service you're providing.** You shouldn't expect any ticker tape parades in your honor, or a monument being erected of you in your home town. But that's okay. The fact is that **you are touching more lives and influencing more people in a positive manner** than most people do in most other occupations. If you're truly a professional then you're helping people more than most people could ever even dream about. You're what I call a high impact person. You impact people by getting them to make good decisions. You impact people by getting them to do things that will make a lasting difference in their lives. You're impacting America by keeping your country growing because nothing happens until a sale is made.

Recently I read an excerpt from a book by Leo Buscaglia called *Born for Love*. I immediately thought of the good ethical salesperson when I read his message. Here's the quote, "The majority of us lead quiet, unheralded lives as we pass through this world...there are scores of people waiting for someone just like us to come along; people who will appreciate our compassion, our encouragement, who will need our unique talents. Someone who will live a happier life merely because we took the time to share what we had to give. Too often we underestimate the power of a touch, a smile, a kind word, a listening ear, an honest compliment, or the smallest act of caring, all of which have the potential to turn a life around. It's overwhelming to consider the continuous opportunities there are to make our love felt."

If you are good at what you do, than you're making your love felt through your life's calling. **You are making a difference in the hundreds of families and businesses you visit and serve.** No, there probably will not be a ground swell to erect that monument in your honor, nor will people be lining up to get your autograph, but **you can certainly feel very good about what you're doing.** A sales career is an honorable and admirable profession. It is a calling that deserves your best effort and your honest dealing. You get paid exactly what you deserve—not a penny more nor a penny less. **Always remember that nothing happens until you do your job.** Nothing happens until a sale is made. Think of the people you have helped.

Do you have an image problem? I hope not. There just aren't too many people who can do what you do. **So hold your head high. Be proud of what you do. Know that you are making a difference** in the lives of the families and businesses you serve. Feel good about what you're doing and don't let other people determine your self-esteem. And guess what, they probably couldn't read your autograph anyway. Good luck and happy selling!

Chapter 72

AND THE WINNER IS. . . .

"The careers of many early titans of American industry, like Andrew Carnegie, were marked by spectacular leaps from poverty, hairbreath escapes, bankruptcies, and near bankruptcies, failed products and concepts. Within each broken dream, they learned what they had to learn, dusted themselves off and started over."
—Harvey Mackay

Horatio Alger Jr. graduated from Harvard Divinity School in 1852. He became a Unitarian minister. He also became a writer and author. It was said that he became the preacher of the "Gospel of success". Virtually all of his books had a rags-to-riches theme. He wrote over 100 books and sold more than 20,000,000 copies. His most famous books were: *Ragged Dick*, *Luck and Pluck* (with my name I think I should have authored both of those), and *Tattered Tom*. His books preached that by **honesty, cheerful perseverance, and hard work**, the poor but virtuous would have their just reward—though the reward was almost always precipitated by a stroke of good luck. Today, the Horatio Alger Award is still presented annually to someone with a "rags to riches" success experience.

My Dad has often used the expression, "I'd rather be lucky than good." I've often debated that statement, but never convincingly enough for him. Me, **I'd rather be lucky and good!** Where exactly does luck enter into the formula for success? A very successful Agent in the company I work for often uses this statement, **"The harder I work, the luckier I get."** Now that's good! The chances of getting lucky by contacting a person who just happens to need your product or service is much greater if you talk to one hundred people than it is if you talk to only five. The harder you work; the luckier you'll get. The logic is undeniable.

Once you've been in a sales position for a while (how long will vary by type of product or service), most people develop the ability to sell. If you are good with people, if you can demonstrate empathy and build trust, and if people have a need for your product or service, sooner or later you're going to make a sale with them. Hence the statement I make to people in our Agency, **"People fail in our business not so much for the people they don't sell, as the people they don't see!"** If you see enough people, sooner or later someone will make a mistake and buy! It's almost that simple! You could be consciously incompetent in your area of sales, and yet if you called on enough people, you would make some sales. After all, as the saying goes, "Even a blind pig roots up an ear of corn once in a while."

The qualities that Horatio Alger Jr. zeroed in on are quite interesting. **Honesty. Cheerful perseverance. Hard work.** Those qualities have certainly stood the test of time, haven't they? They are as important today in selling and in life as they were back in the mid 1800's. How could anyone expect to become a long term sucess unless they were completely honest? Looking someone in the eye and telling them both the pros and cons, the good features and the drawbacks to a product, will do more to sell your prospects on you than almost anything else you can do. It's pretty tough to look someone in the eye and lie to them, isn't it? You recognize the word perseverance in sales immediately. Perseverance is pleasant and polite persistence. Probably more has been written about perseverance in these messages than almost any other word. But notice the adjective "cheerful" ahead of it. People like doing business with a friend. **People like doing business with someone who is pleasant, friendly, and generally happy.** It sure makes for a better relationship! Smile seems to deserve some recognition here. Be pleasant and accommodating. Apply the Golden Rule and see how people will respond. And a good work ethic almost goes without saying. It certainly goes hand in hand with success.

Honesty, cheerful perseverance and hard work. Great ingredients in any success formula. Horatio Alger Jr., in effect, was telling us that with these values and virtues, good luck is almost sure to follow. Maybe not today or tomorrow, but over time they are ingredients that will dictate a successful life. Do you possess them? If you do, someday you may hear your name being called during this announcement, "And the winner of this year's Horatio Alger Award is_____!" Will you have been lucky? Maybe. **But with honesty, cheerful perseverance and hard work, your chances of being lucky increase dramatically!** It pays to be both lucky and good!

Chapter 73

CAVEAT EMPTOR—
LET THE BUYER BEWARE

"The customer is always right...sometimes confused, misinformed, rude, stubborn, changeable and even downright stupid...but never wrong."
—Executive Speechwriter Newsletter
Volume 8 Number 4

Caveat emptor. No wonder Latin is dead! Caveat emptor is as obsolete an idea as the notion that the world was coming to an end in 1975. If you are in a sales position today and have "caveat emptor" as a philosophy—you'd better start looking for a new career or a time machine that will transport you back to the early 1900's.

Caveat emptor is a fairly familiar Latin phrase. The phrase can be traced all the way back to 1054. The entire expression is actually "Caveat emptor Quisa ignorare non debuit quod jus alienum emit", which means, "Let the buyer beware because he should not be ignorant of the property that he is buying" (as my eight year old nephew, Matt, would say, "I knew that!").

Today, caveat emptor should have no place in our culture. At one time the plight of a transaction depended on the buyer's resourcefulness and thoroughness in looking for defects, "lemons" and other product deficiencies. Today we operate in an entirely different environment. Things have changed. Consumer protection agencies and consumer advocate groups have lobbied long and hard on the consumer's behalf. Progress has been made so that poor workmanship, improperly performing products and products that don't hold up to their claims, will not be acceptable and will entitle consumers to a refund of their money or a replacement of their product. Actually, it should never come to that. Your customers should never be placed in a position that will lead to anything less than their complete satisfaction.

Today the buyer has all the power. The information age has allowed buyers everywhere access to volumes of information about a variety of products and services. Global markets now provide competition in almost every area of goods and services. The world has shrunk to the point where you are only seconds away from the most distant seller via E-Mail, Fax machines, and 800 numbers. Market niches have arisen from products and services that only five or six years ago were market niches themselves. We live in an age of specialization and customization. No more **"one size fits all" but rather customize and personalize.** The buyer is in fact, king. Caveat emptor? Not on your life!

So how do you proceed as a salesperson? **In a word—relationships.** Through constant improvement, constant quality service, and constant differentiation, you win customer loyalty by building a solid relationship.

Let's talk about the first one—**constant improvement.** Improvement needs to take place on two levels. First, product or service improvement. You normally must rely on your company to be on the ball here, with frequent innovations, upgrades, and improvements. Second, **you need to constantly improve the relationship.** Sending an article you saw that might be of interest is a way of improving customer relationships. So is periodic contacts to see if the customer is satisfied or needs something. Tickets to an "event" like sports or the theater also help to solidify the relationship. **You must constantly find ways to improve your relationship.** If a customer becomes a friend, it's going to be pretty tough for a competitor to gain the upper hand.

The second area is **constant quality service.** Since people demand and expect more today, you have to provide it and then some. Go the extra mile for your customers and exceed their expectations. Anticipate their needs. **Spoil them with good service.** Make sure that TQM—Total Quality Management—isn't just a fad, but a way of life.

Finally, the third area is **constant differentiation.** Always, always find **ways to differentiate yourself from your competition.** Do lots of little things just a little bit better than your competition is doing. A typed written Agenda for each meeting is one way of showing you are different, you're organized, and you respect their time. Maybe it's giving a fancy wallet or folder for a policy or contract. Or a plaque that identifies them as an outstanding customer of yours. Perhaps it's a painting or a furnishing you purchase for their office. It could even be offering to make a presentation to their boss or board of directors. **Find out what it is that will surely differentiate yourself from your competition, then do it!**

Caveat emptor has had its day. Why it had its day is hard to imagine. The salesperson with that philosophy obviously had no inclination toward repeat sales or building a relationship. Today, as a salesperson **you'd better be ready to provide satisfaction guaranteed or your money back. Then provide constant improvement, superior service**

and constant differentiation from your competition. When you do those things, you'll be establishing a solid relationship built on trust, mutual respect and unending loyalty. And watch out or you're just liable to turn that customer into a friend.

Chapter 74

NO PAIN; NO GAIN

"We all must suffer one of two pains; the pain of discipline or the pain of regret."

—Steve Kramnick

Well said! **Discipline is making yourself do the right things at the right times.** And yes, sometimes it is painful. As painful as it is, however, it's still less painful in the end, than failure and the pain of regret. Success simply exacts a price that has to be paid. It's never easy. Sacrifices have to be made. Fears must to be conquered. Unpleasant tasks need to be tackled. Discipline is what usually separates the successful person from the unsuccessful person. Discipline is what makes **the successful person do what the unsuccessful person will simply not do.** Discipline is making yourself do the unpleasant task when it's time to do it. In our business, and most sales careers, it usually centers around telephoning for appointments. That's usually the least enjoyable activity a salesperson is asked to do.

It is easy to read e-mail messages from the Home Office, or study a chapter of a training manual, or prepare for an interview when, in fact, it's time to get on the telephone. In the end, however, that will be a painful and costly decision. It is very easy to delude yourself into thinking that you're working hard, especially when you stay busy with a bevy of business activities. The reality of our business is that **there are only two events**

which are both urgent and important—seeing the people and attempting to see the people. Everything else is a distant third. The pain of discipline involves controlling those two "main event" activities in order to experience the gain (i.e. success).

Is it worth it? While you must answer that question for yourself, here's what Steve Kramnick said, "We all must suffer one of two pains; the pain of discipline or the pain of regret. **The pain of discipline weighs ounces whereas the pain of regret weighs tons.**" How interesting! The pain of discipline pales in comparison to the pain of regret. Can you relate to that? I certainly can. When I have procrastinated tackling a problem, the problem usually becomes even greater, causing regret and in the end more pain.

Sometimes I think we make this business of sales harder than it needs to be. We know what it takes to be successful—seeing the people. Today, **there's no doubt that the challenge of seeing people is greater than ever before.** If that's the case then we need even more discipline than normal. If we take time to plan and put some systems into place we can help ourselves to be more disciplined.

Planning and setting up all your phone time for the week seems pretty basic. Yet, time and again I'd have to say not many salespeople do that. As a result we meander through the week and end up experiencing the pain of regret. All of a sudden we remark, "Boy, where did this week go to?" or "Wow, I sure didn't do the things I wanted to do this week!" "I just couldn't find time to phone for appointments this week." All of these very natural responses mean that you will be experiencing the pain of regret and it's likely to affect your production for weeks to come. **If you want to experience the "gain"**

badly enough, then the pain of discipline is definitely the way to go. Ounces are definitely better than tons. Better to experience the pain of discipline than the pain of regret. You can experience the pain of discipline by doing the following four things:

1. **Plan your week. Be as specific and intentional as you can possibly be.** Make sure you have "telephoning" a couple times every single day. I've said it before but it bears repeating "life's a cinch by the inch but hard by the yard".

2. Get in the habit this week of **not letting anything (and I do mean anything!) interfere with your telephone time.** That's sacred time. It's your lifeblood. Miss one telephone time period and you will suffer the pain of regret for weeks.

3. **Keep score. Measurement will always improve performance.** Play mental games with yourself and watch yourself improve. Go for the record (number of appointments) once in a while.

4. **Reward yourself for your successes.** This is a mental business. If your goal was to contact ten people during the twenty minutes of phone time, and you did it, then reward yourself somehow. Figure out what works for you. What keeps you motivated to do the tough stuff? If you can answer that question you should have glimpses of what you can do to endure the pain of discipline by making the phone calls.

Discipline is never easy. If it were, there would be a lot more successful people in sales today. Most people simply lack the chutzpah to discipline themselves in order to be successful. **If you're willing to endure the pain of discipline, you will not have to worry about the pain of regret.** And the gain is definitely worth it!

Chapter 75

GRANDMOTHERS ARE SPECIAL PEOPLE

"Life is made up, not of great sacrifices or duties, but of little things in which smiles and kindness and small obligations given habitually, are what win and preserve the heart and secure comfort."
— Sir Humphry Davy

Both my Grandmothers died when I was fairly young. That was too bad. They were both neat ladies. Unfortunately, I was too young to really appreciate them. They were both nurturers and encouragers. They were kind. Non-judgmental. Accepting. Loving. Looking back, they had a very positive influence on me and I loved them.

Grandmothers are special people. They can look past all the little irritable things grandchildren do, and focus on the cute and adorable things. How refreshing! What a concept! We can sure learn a lot from them. If everyone were more 'Grandmother-like' what better relationships we would experience. What a difference it would make!

Are you a nurturer and an encourager? Or do people think of you as a drill sergeant? Much of society today is bent on confrontation. There seems to be an "in your face" mentality that tends to tear down relationships rather than building them up. Humor tends to be sarcastic, dry, caustic. A cross somewhere between Bob Newhart and Don Rickles (or Jerry Seinfeld and Dice Clay for you younger people). People apparently have the notion that if they put someone else down, they themselves are somehow elevated. To me it stems from low self-esteem and is certainly immature if not defensive behavior.

I don't know about you, but I respond very positively to *warm fuzzies*. If someone says some flattering things about me, I feel like a million bucks! If someone tells me what a great job I did for them, I'm ready to do more. Throw a few compliments my way and I'm ready to *walk through fire* for them. Oh, I may blush a little when I'm complimented in front of others, but I love it! Those "strokes" we receive are wonderful. They build our egos and our self-esteem. It's like water to a flower. They give us confidence and encourage us to do more. **Grandmother-like behavior by those around us leads to blossoming relationships.**

Grandmothers are indeed special people. They could give lectures to all of us on building relationships. They could entitle it Psychology 101:

Look for the good in people.

Be quick to praise.

Catch them "doing something right".

Give people reasons to feel good about themselves. Build them up.

Constantly accentuate their strengths.

Let them know they're important.

Compliment them often.

Applaud their efforts.

Empathize with them.

Water them and watch them blossom.

Fortunately, Grandmothers don't lecture us; they simply live their lectures by demonstrating all of the above.

We could all use more Grandmothers in our lives. People who build us up and nurture us. Friends who will encourage us and see the good in us even at times when we're "down" or not doing our best. If you don't have many "Grandmothers" in your life right now, seek some out. Spend more time with people who build you up and less time with people who criticize you. **Spend more time with people who nurture you and less time with people who berate you.** More time with people who encourage you and less time with people who nag you. What is the best way to solicit that type of behavior and relationship? Be more Grandmother-like yourself. Remember, what goes around comes around. **People can't help liking you and encouraging you, when you're busy nurturing and encouraging them.** No matter how old you are or what sex you are, be Grandmother-like—they're special people.

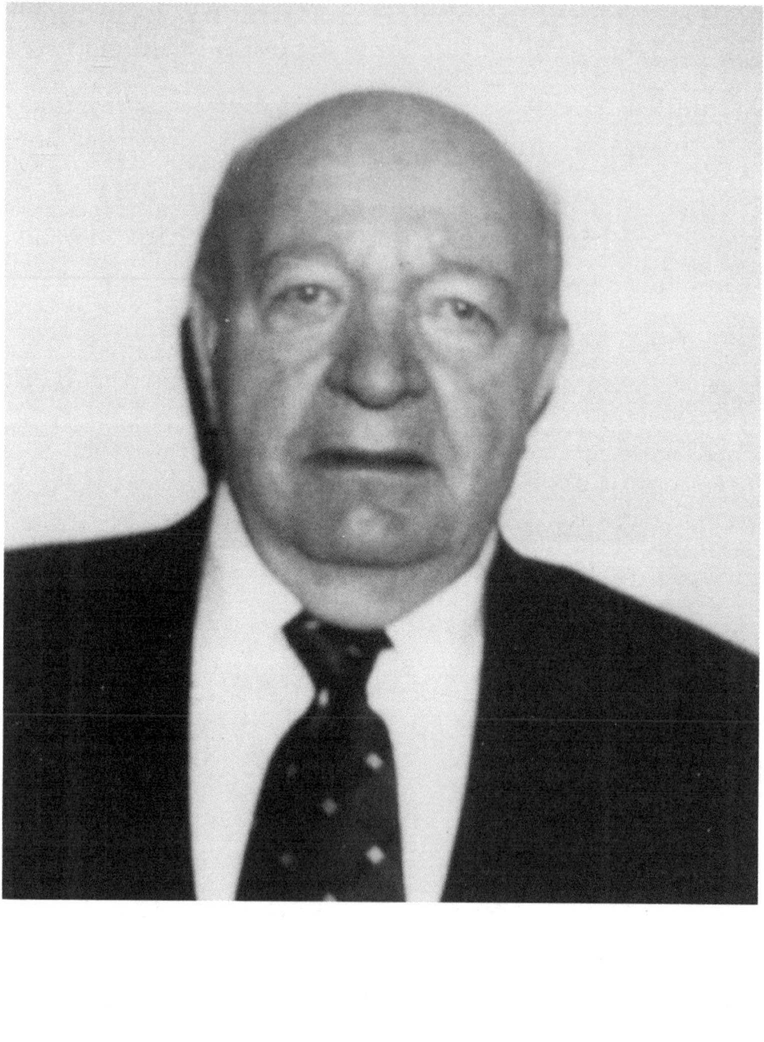

THIS CHAPTER IS DEDICATED
ROY WENLAND

Roy Wenland is a big man in many ways. His gruff outward appearance, loud booming voice and physical stature may intimidate many people, but they all belie the fact that he has a heart of gold. In fact, half his weight may be his heart! He has been a friend of mine for over 30 years and has been a real blessing to me and to my family. It's a real pleasure for me to acknowledge him, honor him, and thank him for the positive influence he's been in my life.

Roy was an assistant football coach when I was in high school. He was not a teacher at Lutheran West in Rocky River, Ohio. He had two daughters who attended school there. He was not compensated for his coaching. He simply loved the game and volunteered to help. He wasn't the most popular coach because he worked the players hard and drove them relentlessly. He always demanded a player's best and would accept nothing less. That toughness and determination, while admirable traits, did not win him many popularity contests. But even then, below that exterior of his, you got glimpses of the real Roy Wenland. He would do anything for you. Roy followed my football career at West Point, attended a couple of games we played at Pittsburgh, and even attended my graduation. We even managed to go to a couple of Army-Navy games together when we lived in Allentown, PA. His role in my life has always been one of fierce, loyal support. Our friendship has deepened over the years, sometimes through adversity like the loss of a loved one, sometimes through visits, sometimes through letters and phone calls. We stay in touch even after all these years.

Roy's daughter, Peggy, was our son Reed's godmother until God called her home a few years ago. His other daughter, Judy, picked up right where Peggy left off. Roy, you have honored me with your interest, your caring and your friendship. You have encouraged me and supported me for all these years. I know I haven't said, "Thank you" enough and haven't told you how much your caring and love have meant to me. I only hope you know what a positive influence you have been in my life and how much I care for you. I love you!

Dick

Chapter 76

COURAGE

"Courage, the highest gift, that scorns to bend to mean devices for a sordid end, Courage — an independent spark from Heaven's bright throne, By which the soul stands raised, triumphant, high alone."
— George Farguhar

There's one word I've never heard Sales Managers mention when talking about recruiting and selecting the right salesperson. It's a word which is often overlooked and frequently underrated. Yet, every successful salesperson has it. It comes in different forms; it comes in all different sizes and shapes. If this one word wasn't a necessary ingredient to perform the various tasks which salespeople must complete, then the compensation for their work would be much less. The fact is that most people couldn't do the things salespeople do. Have you guessed the word yet? Of course you have, you've read the title of this chapter. The word is courage.

It takes courage to be a successful salesperson and do what you do. It takes courage to risk being rejected time and time again. It takes courage to get up after being knocked down, dust yourself off and try again. It takes courage too, to start new ventures and try new ideas and new marketing approaches. It takes what the Jewish people call "chutzpah"! One of the best definitions of chutzpah I've heard is this: **"He who owns his own spurs"**. People who have courage have their own initiative and drive to get the job done. They are willing to hear people say "No!" to them again and again because they're convinced that it brings them that much closer to their next "Yes!". They don't take the rejection personally, they simply take it as part of the job—a necessary evil. While some people would stop trying after a certain amount of rejection, the courageous salesperson works on, knowing full well that sooner or later someone will buy. You don't need to have the cheapest product. You don't need to have the highest quality product available. You don't need to be offering the best "deal". If you see enough people, someone will indeed have a need which you can fill.

When I started in my sales career over twenty years ago, I received this friendly advice tongue in cheek: "Dick, just see enough people and sooner or later someone will make a mistake and buy." While the comment was meant to be humorous there is an awful lot of truth to that statement. Early on in a professional sales career when a person's knowledge of their product isn't all that great (let alone knowledge about the competition), they often luck into sales because they just happen to be in the right place at the right time. **Isn't it interesting that it happens more to the people who really hustle and see the most people than to those who don't?** Indeed, it takes courage to handle rejection and keep going.

There are many types of courage. It takes a certain type of courage to go into battle when your life is on the line. It takes another type of courage to overcome feelings of anxiety when facing an unpleasant task. When people have been surveyed and asked what scares them the most, fear of public speaking usually ranks number one, even above fear of dying. To get up in front of people, therefore, takes a certain type of courage.

People in a sales position generally have to be great risk takers. That takes courage! If you don't pick up the phone and ask someone for an appointment, you will not experience rejection. Of course, you won't have any sales either! **The bottom line in sales positions is that you have to make many attempts in order to be successful.** That takes chutzpah or courage.

Courage? If you're in sales, you know what it's all about. You need it every day in your business not only to survive but to succeed. Here are three things you can do to continue to cultivate this important ingredient:

1. **Let your goal be your beacon in the night.** No matter what problems are strewn in your path, remain fixed on your goal. Let it be your driving force and your catalyst to keep going. Don't let the little things distract you.

2. **Remember that you cannot control all the variables that go into a sale.** Concentrate only on the variables that you can control. You cannot control whether one particular prospect will say "Yes", but you can control your preparation and professional presentation. And you can control the number of people you ask every week to make a buying decision.

3. **Recall past successes and visualize a repeat performance.** Nothing breeds success like success. Success creates confidence, and fosters even greater courage.

I hope you realize just how courageous you really are. Don't be held back by the cynics or skeptics who will never accomplish great things and relish the notion that they are the conscience of salespeople. Rather, reach for the stars with all the courage you can muster. **Focus on your goal, control the variables within your power and be nurtured by your past suc-**

cesses. Then, watch your courage soar! Give yourself credit for the courage you possess because very few people could do what you do.

Chapter 77

LOOKING THE PART

When asked why he showed up for a football game in a black pin-striped, vested suit, assistant-football coach Bob Borkowski replied, "I wanted to look nice if we won, and if we lost this would be nice to be buried in."

When I was in grade school and high school I had a great part-time job. It started out to be washing windows at a local barber shop. Later it developed into a weekend job where my older brother and I would clean the whole barber shop. We could do it any time Saturday night, Sunday or even Monday since it was closed that day too. We dusted, swept, mopped, cleaned ashtrays, mirrors, sinks and, yes, even the toilets. It was flexible hours, steady pay, radio and TV at our disposal and even a fringe benefit of giving an occasional haircut to each other (ouch!). It was a great job! That's where I was when I saw Lee Harvey Oswald get shot. Even today when I hear certain songs on the "oldies" station, I immediately think of the barber shop. Our boss was a very generous man. He trusted us completely and tipped us rather handsomely at holiday time. When my brother went to West Point my best friend took his place and we did that job together for a number of years. I even used the barber shop as a secret rendezvous spot with my then girlfriend (now wife).

The place had four barbers. The father who was the original owner, the son, who was our boss, and there were two other barbers. The father was in the twilight of his career and gave very few haircuts—only to a few of his regular customers. Most professional men sat and waited for our boss who probably gave the best haircuts. My favorite barber was Jim. He was usually pretty busy too, but most of all was just a great guy. And then there was the fourth barber. To say that he was a little rough around the edges is to say that Madonna wears a little makeup. The guy was a slob. He was never clean shaven. He always seemed to be in need of a haircut. He was a sloppy dresser. If you deleted the expletives from his conversation I guess you'd have to say he had little to say. I hope you're getting a mental image that this guy was not a walking billboard for GQ!

Would you walk into that barber shop and go sit in his chair? Not many other people did either. People would wait thirty minutes or more to get a haircut from the boss or Jim while the fourth barber would sit chattering loudly with nothing to do (and not much to say either). Which brings me, finally, to my point—he couldn't sell his haircuts to people who needed haircuts because he didn't project the kind of personal appearance people wanted. People wanted neatness. They wanted to look "spiffy". They wanted a good haircut from someone who took pride in his work and pride in his personal appearance. They wanted conversation that was pleasant and the right volume, not conversation that was loud and raunchy. I knew that before I was even twelve years old! It wasn't rocket scientist stuff.

Do you dress for success? Do you create a great first impression? Will your prospects meet you for the first time and say to themselves, "Now there's a real professional! This is a person I can trust." **The first thirty seconds in front of a prospect may well mean everything.** Here are some things people look for:

1. **Personal Appearance**

    Hair neat and combed;

    Clean shaven or neat and trim mustache or beard;

    Suits preferably to sports coats;

    Wool rather than polyesters;

    Clean and shined shoes;

    Good erect posture;

    A warm and sincere smile;

    Good eye contact;

    Not too much makeup;

    An air of confidence.

2. **Manners**

    Firm handshake;

    Wearing overshoes or boots when the weather warrants it;

    Not removing overcoat until invited to;

    Not sitting down until invited to;

    For men, rising when someone else enters the room;

    Not interrupting people when they are speaking;

    Not overextending your time;

    Being polite and courteous at all times.

3. **Communicative skills**

    Listening more; talking less;

    Maintaining good eye contact;

    Talking "with" rather than "at" or worse yet "down" to your prospects;

Never using abbreviations common to your business (you lose credibility if your customers don't understand it);

Never asking the prospect if they understand something but taking the responsibility for explaining it clearly;

Using silence effectively;

Asking your prospect to elaborate more or asking them why that is important to them;

Using proper grammar! Brush up on your language usage (verbs today especially-come vs. came, don't vs. doesn't);

Avoid trite and repetitious phrases like "you know";

Use humor when it's appropriate (Never off-color).

It's important now and then to take stock of how you're doing. Do you always make a good first impression? Do you create a scenario where people will want to work with you?. Are you fun to be with? Can you become a friend to people? **Remember to exude confidence and enthusiasm.** Those two things will do a lot to sell any product. Warmth and a sincere smile also go a long way. You must also believe in your product and project that belief. Prospects want to do business **with people who project an image of how they expect a salesperson to look and act like.** Looking the part could make all the difference in the world in making that great first impression.

Chapter 78

"I WILL ACT NOW"*

"In any moment of decision the best thing you can do is the right thing. The next best thing is the wrong thing and the worst thing you can do is nothing."
—Theodore Roosevelt

Procrastination is a nasty word. It denotes a lack of responsibility—dereliction of duty. **It is simply the act of postponing.** It's staying on the sideline rather than being in the game. It's putting off till tomorrow what should be done today. One thing is for sure—we've all been guilty of it at times in our lives. It's easy to postpone doing an unpleasant duty, task or responsibility. We convince ourselves that there's no harm done. The problem of procrastination can actually get worse as we get older, too! Why? Because as we get older we have fewer people we have to answer to—less accountability. So the opportunity to procrastinate becomes greater and greater. Pretty soon we've accepted passage to Someday Isle. Someday I'll get around to cleaning the garage. Someday I'll fix that broken handle. Someday I'll take care of that service work the customer called about.

Only action will help us accomplish our goals. Only action will allow us to grow and develop. Only action will allow us to risk and fail and bounce up again and succeed. Are you in the game or on the sidelines? Does the question disturb you? Have you become an expert at figuring out excuses not to do something right away? Are you staying in your comfort zone

253

too much? Are you procrastinating by not risking a little more often? **Act now!** As Bo Jackson used to say, "Just do it!" We must be bold in our action and hunger for success. We must persist again and again and not accept failures and setbacks. We must be willing to act and we must do it now!

Here are some practical things that may help you in dealing with procrastination:

1. **Break down big goals or big tasks into small steps which can be accomplished in small time periods.** The Chinese proverb, "The journey of a thousand miles begins with one step" gives good insight into this solution. And, of course, the answer to the question, "How do you eat an elephant?" is "One bite at a time."

2. **Prioritize your "To Do" list and give yourself deadlines.** By doing this you'll at least be doing the most important things first.

3. **Don't become distraught or "sidelined" by setbacks or other distractions.** Expect them. Anticipate them. Act now and finish the task.

4. **Don't beat yourself up mentally for procrastinating once in a while.** You're human. We've all been there. When you recognize that you're doing it, give yourself a deadline and stick to it. Then give yourself a mental pat on the back when you finish it!

5. **Don't think something has to be just perfect before you try doing it.** Just do it —and do it now! That certainly doesn't mean preparation isn't important and necessary. It just means that there is a big difference between thinking about doing something and actually doing it!

Do you hunger for success? Success will not wait. Don't wait for your ship to come in, swim out to it! Act now! **Act now and avoid the debilitating effect of procrastination.** Johann Wolfgang von Goethe once wrote, "Are you in earnest? Seize this very minute. What you can do, or dream you can, begin it. Boldness has genius, power and magic in it. Only engage and the mind grows heated; Begin and then the work will be completed." Don't procrastinate. Act now!

* The title of the Scroll Marked IX from Og Mandino's classic best seller, *The Greatest Salesman in the World*, Lifetime Books Publisher

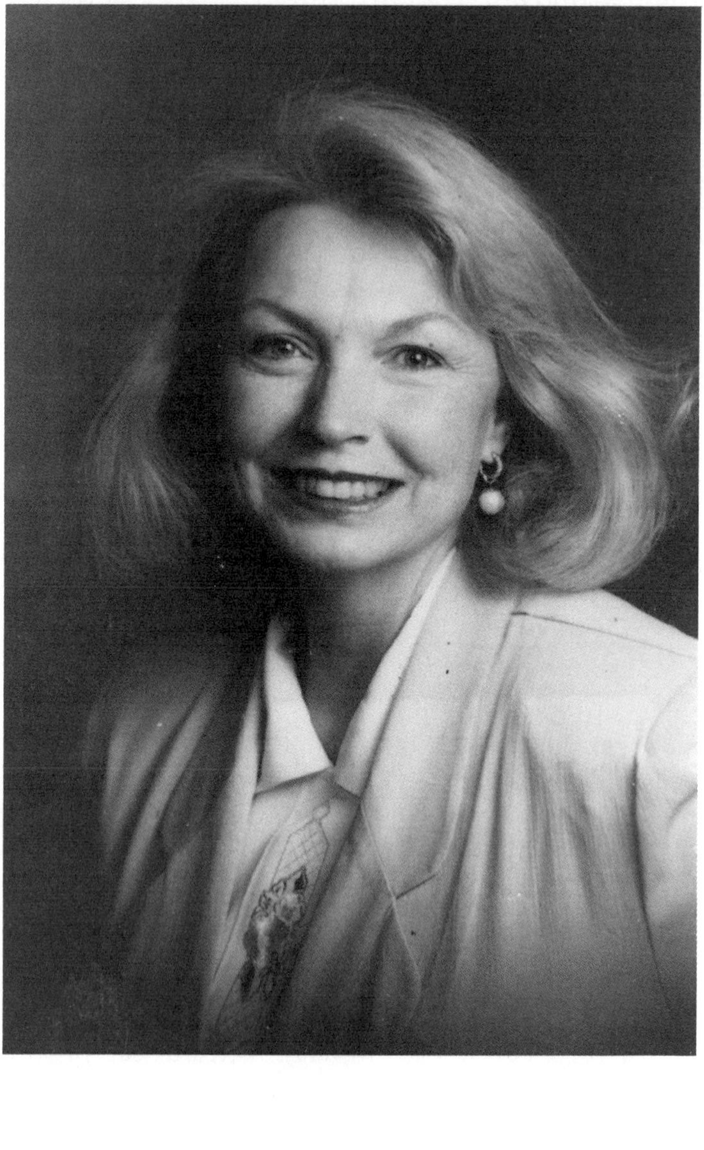

THIS CHAPTER IS DEDICATED TO
LINDA LUECKE

In the sixth grade you entered my life and it's made all the difference in the world. By the time we were juniors in high school you had won my affection and my heart. That was over 33 years ago. It seems like only yesterday! The emotional love for you that I experienced then has continued to grow, continued to mature and continued to flourish. The girl I loved then has blossomed into the most gracious, beautiful and caring woman that I know. My marriage to you twenty seven years ago (June 15, 1969) shall always remain the most important event in my life.

You define what love is for me. All comparisons begin and end with you. You were the first woman I ever loved and today you remain the only woman I have ever loved. You know my philosophy, "Why settle for hamburger when you have steak at home!" You are indeed my most cherished possession and my richest blessing. Quite simply, I adore you!

You have a spark about you and a personality that makes people feel better when they are with you. Your contagious smile is a mere glimpse of the beautiful person you are both inside and out. You care about people and you feel for people. You have a capacity to love that I can only marvel at and attempt to emulate.Twenty seven years ago when we took our wedding vows, I could not have imagined nor predicted what we have experienced together. You represent all that is good to me. You have given me joy and happiness beyond my wildest expectations. I know of no happier couple. There have been no rocky roads nor rough spots. There has never been one moment when I have regretted marrying you. I love you today more than ever before. My respect and admiration for you continues to grow daily. To me, you are the best! We hardly ever have "words" with each other and only two "major discussions" (red wig, horseshoe pits). In twenty seven years that's not bad! You are my best roommate ever!

Thank you for twenty seven great years. Thank you for helping me the many ways you do. Thank you for supporting me and nurturing me. Thanks for being my biggest fan. You have influenced me far more than anyone else in my life. Thank you for sacrificing your career in order to help raise our three sons. Thank you for being a loving mother. Thank you for putting up with crazy schedules and hectic days. But mainly, thank you for loving me the way you do. You put that smile on my face. I will always bask in your warmth and your love. When I thank God for the blessings He has given me, I begin and end with you. I pledge to you once again all my love and faithfulness "till death us do part".

Dick

Chapter 79

THE BUCK STOPS HERE

"The men who succeed best in public life are those who take the risk of standing by their own convictions."
—James A. Garfield
Twentieth President

You recognize the title immediately if you're forty-five or older. Harry Truman had it indelibly etched on a paper weight which sat on his desk when he was President of the United States. It was a constant reminder to him that he was totally responsible for his decisions and had no one else to blame for failures.

You gotta love that phrase! "The buck stops here!" **It's taking total responsibility for everything that happens to you.** It's still a great philosophy for all of us in sales today. Don't blame any of your failures on your company, or the economy, or your products, or the market. No excuses accepted! Rather, **take total responsibility for your results, whether they be successes or failures.** That's taking ownership of your problems and making the assumption that you're the person responsible. What are the benefits of this philosophy?

1. **You will take your decisions and choices more seriously** when you realize they have consequences.

2. **You will learn to control the variables that you have the ability to control** and not to worry about the rest.

3. **You will not waste your time blaming others** but rather use it creatively to overcome obstacles that are keeping you from being successful.

4. It enables you to accept the notion that you are in **control and the master of your destiny.** Adversity and setbacks are a natural phenomenon in this adventure called life. There are many events and issues that are absolutely out of your control. But **"the buck stops here" philosophy empowers you to decide once and for all that you are ultimately in control of your overall success or failure.**

There have been times in my life when I have felt out of control—when it seemed like things were changing and happening so fast around me that I didn't control my own destiny. That's not unusual. But that should always be a temporary situation and not a permanent one. That should always be caused by unusual circumstances and not be a way of life. The sooner you can gain control of the situation and once again take total responsibility with "the buck stops here" philosophy, the better off you will be. It's also healthy, proper and right to recognize that the Master Planner, God Himself, is really in charge. He's really calling all the shots. Asking Him for help is not only smart but suitable and proper.

President Harry Truman had this sign on his desk at a time when he was faced with a very monumental decision. You probably know it was whether or not he should order the dropping of the atomic bomb on Hiroshima, Japan. Pretty heavy stuff indeed! Ultimately it was his decision and his decision alone. His philosophy held him in good stead. He did make that tough decision and took total responsibility for it.

There hasn't been near that kind of pressure and stress that I have incurred on any major decision I have had to make in my lifetime. I'd like to think that is also true of all the readers. Most decisions we make are not life and death situations. There are important decisions and decisions which will definitely have major consequences, but not the kind that would measure up to the one that Harry Truman had to make. So take heart. Weigh the consequences, debate the options and choices, pray to God for wisdom and understanding and then make your decision. But no matter what the results are, **accept the responsibility of the decision because remember, "the buck stops here"!**

Chapter 80

A BLINDING GLIMPSE OF THE OBVIOUS

"Don't search for opportunities in a distance until you have exhausted the advantages of those right where you are."
—Jerry L. Jones, Sr.

Every once in a while I'll be looking for something very frantically only to find out it was almost right in front of me to begin with. Ever happen to you? It occurred to me that's like coming to some grand conclusion on something which should have been very obvious to begin with. It's like a blinding glimpse of the obvious.

There are many selling techniques, sales tips and relationship issues which could be labeled "a blinding glimpse of the obvious." While the following may be obvious to you, it never hurts to **intentionally** review some basic and "obvious" good ideas:

- Negative manipulation is very harmful to building long term relationships;
- You're only given one chance to make a good first impression;
- If you're telling, you're not selling;
- **Eye contact builds trust in a relationship;**
- Keeping people informed after the sale is the first opportunity to demonstrate your commitment to service;
- **Every attempt to differentiate yourself from your competition will be rewarded with greater loyalty by your customers;**

- The more information you have about your prospects prior to a meeting, the better prepared you can be to meet their expectations;
- Just like a leopard can't change its spots, people seldom change their personalities;
- Mirroring your customers rate of speech will make them feel more comfortable;
- Smiling sincerely will project warmth and build a better relationship;
- Having an application/order form already partially filled out demonstrates your confidence in your proposal;
- The more consistent your behavior, the more people will be able to "read" where you're coming from;
- Silence allows your customers an opportunity to **provide more information;**
- **Your enthusiasm for your recommendations will go a long way toward "selling" your customers;**
- Many people today still make emotional buying decisions;
- **Personalizing your presentation to each specific customer** is not only necessary but critical for success;
- Tackle an unpleasant task immediately;
- Paying attention to all the small details is essential for providing quality service to your customers;
- **Always give your customers an opportunity to vote** (i.e. don't forget to ask for the order);
- If you win the battle but lose the war with customers, you'll never have the opportunity to develop a long term relationship;
- You're never too old to learn. **Learning is a lifetime commitment;**

- Others may be smarter; but no one should outwork you;
- **Integrity should be maintained at all costs;**
- Learning the difference between what is important and what seems to be urgent will help you establish proper priorities;
- Procrastinating creates mountains out of molehills;
- Always talk "to" and "with" customers, not down at them;
- KISS - Keep It Simple and Sincere is one of those time honored traditions worth keeping;
- It's not a question of whether we will have obstacles in our lives, but what we do with them once we have them;
- While your parents, sales manager, spouse, and mentors all want you to do well, your own determination alone will be the primary reason whether or not you succeed;
- Questions are your greatest tools in successful selling;
- Proper planning prevents pitfalls;
- **The harder you work the luckier you'll get;**
- Everyone has enough ability to succeed if they have enough determination to succeed;
- Customers "buy" you first, then your company, then your products. Remembering to sell in that order is important;
- An objection is never a "no" but only a request for more information;
- Developing a thick skin when it comes to rejection is vital for your own mental health;
- **When you see or hear "buying" signals, stop selling;**
- There are always opportunities in any situation;

- Failure is never fatal unless you allow it to be final;
- **When you risk more often your chances of succeeding increase exponentially;**
- You can learn something from everyone. After all, even the worst person can serve as a bad example;
- Remaining open to criticism allows for improvement and growth;
- **Success breeds failure unless you remain open to change;**
- By constantly differentiating yourself from your competition you will be building impregnable relationships with your customers;
- **High expectations will lead to lofty accomplishments;**
- Most people are not overnight successes. Success belongs to those who persevere;
- It's less costly in both time and money to retain a good customer than it is to attract a new one;
- **Always think long term;**
- If you don't implement a new idea almost immediately you'll probably lose it;
- Questioning everything you do is healthy and imperative for growth and change.

Basic stuff? Maybe. But even the pros review the basics. Remember Vince Lombardi's opening practice the next season after winning the first ever Superbowl? "Gentleman, this is a football . . . " Maybe a blinding glimpse of the obvious has helped you remember something you used to do but have stopped doing. Maybe it's even gotten you a little excited about trying something new. Great! Just maybe a blinding glimpse of the obvious is what you needed to figure out exactly how to impress that top prospect or customer.

Chapter 81

YOUR VALUABLE TIME

"Time is the coin of your life. It is the only coin you have, and only you can determine how it will be spent. Be careful lest you let other people spend it for you."
—Carl Sandburg

If you're a salesperson then you have lots of different activities. Some of those activities are obviously more important than others. No one should dispute this statement:

The most important time in the salesperson's business life is the time spent in front of prospects and customers.

Everything else pales in comparison. **When you're not in front of a customer or prospect you're basically unemployed.** You cannot make a sale unless you get to see someone (unless of course you do it by phone). While other activites like planning, paperwork, delivery of your product or service, telemarketing and service work are necessary—**they don't compare to face-to-face selling time.**

Do you know how much your selling time is worth? I bet you'd be mighty surprised. If you spend three hours per day in actual face-to-face selling, here's what your time is worth (assuming 250 workdays/year):

If You Earn	An Hour Is Worth
$25,000/yr	$ 33.33
$50,000/yr.	$ 66.66
$75,000/yr.	$ 100.00
$100,000/yr.	$ 133.33

Your face-to-face time is pretty valuable, isn't it? What a great idea to hire someone to do the "other things" so that you can do what you do best—sell! Delegate the "other things" to someone earning $7-12/hr. so that you can spend more time in actual selling interviews. It's one of the most important lessons you should learn. **Paying someone to keep you in front of prospects and customers is also an excellent "investment" into your business.** I challenge you to find a better investment! Hire some key people to keep you doing what you get paid to do. Make it clear to them the valuable role they play in making you more successful. Challenge them to keep you busy in front of prospects and customers. A financial incentive to motivate them would not be out of order. Both time and money are either invested or spent. It's your choice!

Your selling time if very valuable. Increase it incrementally and watch your earnings and profitability increase exponentially.

Chapter 82

ON BEING COACHABLE

"Show me those who want to go to the top, and I'll show you people who will take coaching. They will welcome it. They will beg for it. They will use every God-given talent they have to its utmost. They will drink in inspiration. If they lack desire, they won't work. They won't take coaching."

— Bob Richards

Some people are great at accepting advice, suggestions and constructive criticism. Other people you try to help, accept it about as well as an unsolicited call from an IRS agent at suppertime. Not! Total rejection! You may as well have talked to the wall over there. Ever wonder why? Why are some people so very coachable while others don't seem to have a coachable bone in their body? Does it come naturally to some to be accepting and gracious of help being offered to them? Or is it a learned and acquired trait? Tough questions! I don't pretend to know the answers—only God does. It seems to me, however, that there may be some identifiable reasons why some people are just not very coachable. Some people I suspect are just born "know-it-alls". If you explained to them in great detail the intricate workings of a nuclear power plant, they'd probably nod their head condescendingly as though they knew it all the time. I suspect you know people like that. You can't tell them anything without being rebuffed. Okay, stop the list, that's enough! Others, I speculate, have such low self-esteem they feel it's necessary to "cover for themselves" by defensive behavior. They will reject your ideas and suggestions because they don't want anyone to know they really do need help. Other people are just plain stubborn. They're going to do it their own way no matter what. So, short of a direct order (and even that's questionable), they're going to continue to do it just as they always have "come hell or high water". Still others are just plain immature. They haven't grown up enough to recognize that the more you know, the more you realize that there's so much more you don't know. We're all ignorant—only about different things. So it really doesn't matter to admit you don't know something. As a matter of fact it demonstrates confidence and self-esteem. I'm sure there are lots of other reasons why people are uncoachable. There are many variables at work in our minds so that it would be difficult to pinpoint anyway. We're all different and that's good.

Everyone needs to be coachable, however. There is so much we can learn from each other. Life's too short to spend any amount of time in defensive behavior. How about you? Are you coachable? Before you answer that question, let me explain that my experience has been that most people think they are. Their body language and responses to constructive criticism, however, indicate otherwise. You know the signs. Folded arms or hands on hips. Little direct eye contact. Backward, disinterested lean. Few facial gestures or emotion. Aloofness. They may cut you off before you even finish what you have to say. Quick rebuttal to your ideas or suggestions. Tone that almost screams "Don't tell me"! Cutting, sharp comments that speak volumes about their attitudes toward criticism.

Sometimes being coachable is situational too. Case in point—our three sons. Our sons always seemed to get their coaches nod for being among the most coachable players on their team. Their coaches loved them! One of their football coaches once said, "I wish I had eleven like your son!" That's nice to hear as a parent. Yet advice from good ol' Dad sometimes went in one ear and out the other. Despite all the coaching that I have done over the years and participation in many sports, from our sons' perspective my advice didn't warrant much consideration. What a difference a few years makes though. It's amazing how smart I got from the time they were 18 until they were 23!

Here are some suggestions to improve your "coachability":

1. **Listen intently to suggestions being made;**

2. **Don't prejudge**; don't "pooh-pooh" the ideas being made. Focus on the person offering to help you;

3. **Be "big" enough and confident enough not to be defensive.** Accepting help from someone will foster a better and deeper relationship with that person;

4. **Be gracious. Be patient.** Be appreciative of all suggestions made and advice given. Thank the person genuinely for their help;

5. **Never (!) defend your position.** Never (!) rebuff constructive criticism. You always reserve the right not to heed the advice—but make that decision later. When you defend and rebuff, people will soon stop offering suggestions;

6. **Ultimately, determine what to do with the advice.**

Learn how to improve your coachability. Even Jack Nicklaus in his heyday had a coach. Even when Hammering Hank Aaron was banging out record breaking home runs, he still was counseled by batting instructors. The "great ones" in any walk of life don't claim to have all the answers. Some of them don't even know the questions! But most realize they still have room for improvement. **Listen, demonstrate openness, evaluate the advice, thank the person and decide to implement or not.** There you have it. A short course on coachability! No extra charge. By the way did I tell you I thought you should.....